Praise for Strategies and Tips from a Divorce Coach

"This is the book to buy if you are feeling overwhelmed and fearful that you might not be prepared for divorce. Jennifer Warren Medwin lays out a very clear and comprehensive list of things to do and details not to overlook as you create the organizational foundation for getting through the divorce process. She makes a compelling case for why a Divorce Coach is a great support as a voice of reason and as a practical guide in keeping you focused on all of the actions big and small you need to take care of to get through the divorce. Attorneys are your legal advisors and since divorce is a legal process, they are indispensable. The coach keeps you focused on all of the other details of daily life, helps you plan for the future, and partners with you to maintain an even keel. Give this book to everyone you know who is going through a divorce! Well done, Jennifer!"

Pegotty Cooper, FASAE, IOM, CDC
Founder of Career Strategy Roadmap and
Co-Founder CDC Certified Divorce Coach
Training and Certification
CDC College for Divorce Coaching

"Drawing from her own life experience, education, and her work as a Divorce Coach, Jennifer Warren Medwin has written a must-read book for anyone seeking a more complete understanding of what is necessary and helpful as they prepare for and go through divorce. It normalizes the range of feelings one experiences and facilitates emotional healing using various modalities. She introduces the reader to a variety of avenues for emotional growth and empowerment. The book is flavored with inspirational quotes and informative graphics as well as essential information on the legal, financial, emotional, and organizational parts of the divorce process. This book truly illuminates the advantages of working with a Divorce Coach."

Marsha Cohen, LCSW

"Jennifer Warren Medwin's book is an essential, hands-on guide to help facilitate the many complex factors associated with divorce. Jennifer's guidance is inspirational, informative, and empowering. The valuable tools in her book will build confidence and instill hope for any individual enduring the emotional process of a divorce."

Stacey B. Jones, Ph.D., P.A.
Licensed Psychologist
Gables Psychology and Wellness Associates

"This is a must-read for anyone contemplating a marital dissolution. The book is highly accessible and is packed with practical and concrete recommendations and guidance. It is an invaluable guide in helping people transition into and successfully through one of life's most challenging periods."

Laura Steckler, CFP®, CDFA, CLTC
Senior Vice President, Investments
Managing Director, Investments
Steckler Wealth Management Group

"Jennifer Warren Medwin's book details the value created by having a Divorce Coach by your side when navigating through the legal, financial, and emotional issues that often can cloud objective decision-making when going through divorce. While there are many "how to" or "what to expect" books written about the process of divorce, Jennifer's book stands apart as a one-of-a-kind road map on specific tools offered by a Divorce Coach to a divorcee to help minimize what is often a traumatic and painful process. Having practiced complex matrimonial litigation for 22 years, I would highly recommend this book to both lawyers and as a must-read to anyone considering ending their marriage."

Jason Marks, Esq.
Family Lawyer, Shareholder
Kluger, Kaplan, Silverman, Katzen & Levine P.L.

"As a divorce litigator and having been divorced myself, Jennifer's book is exactly the type of resource that every client needs once they start thinking about divorce. Jennifer's knowledge and passion working as a Divorce Coach comes through on every page. She does a great job of breaking down the divorce process, the different emotions that are felt as someone navigates divorce, and then compassionately delivers advice on how one can implement practices to empower themselves as they go through their divorce journey. The advice and tips that Jennifer offers clients are practical and truly help clients get it right with the support of a Divorce Coach from the onset of their journey. I cannot recommend this book enough — if you are starting the divorce process, this book will help you every — step — of — the — way! If you are a professional that works with divorcing clients — tell them to RUN and get this book NOW. Jennifer, thank you for being the light that so many seek when experiencing divorce."

Sonia Queralt
Co-Founder of Divorceify, Attorney,
Divorce Strategist, & Divorce Survivor

"Jennifer Warren Medwin is an important voice in the call for change in the chaotic world of divorce. For too long, the divorce industry has been centered around the antiquated legal battle when it should be centered around families undergoing what will likely be the most significant and defining life transition. In her book, Jennifer painstakingly provides essential guidance for how to navigate the many layers of the divorce process and to emerge far more empowered and prepared to move forward. Read this book and join the movement to take back control over your life, your transition, and to completely re-script the legacy of divorce."

Storey Jones
dtour.life Founder & CEO

"Wow, Jennifer, thank you for writing this book. For those contemplating divorce, I cannot express how much having a Divorce Coach would have meant to me as I went through my divorce. The stress of divorce kept me numb, and quite frankly, I didn't make the best decisions for myself. I felt as though I was all by myself on a ship in the middle of a big ocean. I just felt so alone. I only wish there had been a book like this for me back then. As a Certified Divorce Coach, Jennifer has created an easy-to-read book to walk you through the many steps you'll be taking over the next few months or even years. With this book, you'll feel that you have a supportive friend standing alongside you on this journey. As you take the time and take in all of the information, you'll be ready to move your life forward in the direction of your dreams, and the stages of divorce and the crazy emotional roller coaster ride you'll be on will be more manageable because of it."

Vicky Townsend, CEO
National Association of Divorce Professionals

"I had the honor of reading Jennifer's book from beginning to end. I have never read such a comprehensive "how to" book, which is full of valuable advice and guidance. Virtually everything someone contemplating a divorce needs to know is mentioned in this book. This is THE tool someone in a life transition phase needs to read to properly organize and plan for their new future."

Robert J. Merlin, Esquire

Robert J. Merlin, P.A.

STRATEGIES AND TIPS FROM A

DIVORCE COACH:
A ROADMAP TO MOVE FORWARD

JENNIFER WARREN MEDWIN, MS, CDC
Certified Divorce Coach®, Certified Marital Mediator,
& Supreme Court of Florida Family Mediator

To request permission, contact the publisher at
veritebooks@gmail.com

Hardcover ISBN: 978-1-7368544-0-2
Paperback ISBN: 978-1-7368544-1-9
E-Book ISBN: 978-1-7368544-2-6

First paperback edition: January 2021

Library of Congress Control Number: 2021925020

Front and back cover by Linda Carta

Edited by: Create 2 Sell & Leah Messing

Book Design by Old Mate Media

Publisher Name: Verite Books

Jennifer Warren Medwin MS, CDC
www.seekingempowerment.com

Change is a positive force that helps you develop. Lean in!

For Jessica and Scott, the two greatest blessings of my life. May you set the intention to speak your truth, make wise choices, and follow your dreams. I love you forever and always!

You matter. Make yourself a priority!

Disclaimer

The information presented in this book is general in nature and not intended to be considered specific or personal advice to any person reading it. Seeking Empowerment Clarity Through Partnership, LLC is a Divorce Coaching and Mediation service. Jennifer Warren Medwin is not an attorney, therapist, or financial advisor and cannot advise you about your specific rights or issues related to your individual matter in these professions. It is the responsibility of each reader to consult with an attorney or another legal professional as needed for legal matters, a therapist regarding mental health issues, and a financial advisor with respect to financial issues. This book should not be your sole source of information.

Nurture yourself and acknowledge how you feel. Take action to cultivate what you want!

Table of Contents

Table of Contents

Honor your truth because denying it does not alter the facts. Tune in and listen to your intuition!

Introduction

Have you ever betrayed your truth? I have. The inner whispers were there from the beginning. At the start of my marriage, the questioning voices spoke softly, and I chose to ignore them. As the years went by, what once were gentle thoughts of doubt, sadness, loneliness, and regret became resounding screams that clouded my thoughts and imprisoned me. I turned into the warden of my own life.

I was conscious of allowing myself to slaughter my soul daily. I wanted out many times, but the fear of what life would be like as a single woman with children paralyzed me. I knew I was not in love with my husband and never really had been. Deep down in my gut, I realized that I was capable and worthy of having more joy and fulfillment in my life. Yet, I allowed my trepidation to keep me stuck. I tried to bury the truth from myself. I knew I was living in a profound state of denial in my relationship.

As much as I tried, I could not really hide from the person I saw and knew in the mirror. The negative feelings of discontent, resentment, and isolation would surface, and I would push them aside. I lived my life on autopilot, hoping things would improve in my marriage but knowing deep down they would not. We had two wonderful children, our health, a very comfortable lifestyle, and close friends. The thought of shattering all that had become the lifeblood of my existence was terrifying. I knew I was slowly dying emotionally, physically, and spiritually in my relationship with my husband; I just didn't want to confront it and questioned my strength.

I allowed fear to imprison me and strip me of joy for too long. Its power over me grew in my unwillingness to move through it and to meet it right where it was. Entering the divorce process, which I resisted, was the biggest challenge of my life. As petrified as I was for my daily routine and family dynamics to change, getting divorced was a gift that thrusted me out of my comfort zone into a world where **my truth** became my foundation.

Through my journey of self-discovery, I learned to reconnect to myself, to push through my own self-betrayal, and to follow my curiosities - I decided to go back to school. My studies focused on the intricacies of the divorce process because I knew, in the depths of my soul, that my journey could have been less complicated emotionally, legally, and ultimately, financially. My goal became to educate clients, frame the divorce process for them, manage their expectations, and most importantly, support them through each step forward. I wanted individuals to experience a more productive and efficient path than I had during the dissolution of my marriage. In time, I became a CDC Certified Divorce Coach®, a Marital Mediator, and a Supreme Court of Florida Family Mediator.

With each brave step I took, the loud voices in my head began to dissipate. I set the intention of connecting to my inner wisdom and personal fulfillment. I walked slowly and mindfully out of the prison I had created for myself. If I can do it, you can do it too!

Possibility is everywhere. Seize the moment!

Section 1

The Divorce Coaching Profession: Demystifying the Big "D"

(©Divorce Coaching Inc. 2011-2021. Used with permission)

Give yourself time. Navigating divorce is a marathon, not a race!

CHAPTER 1

Divorce Coaching Defined by the American Bar Association

"**D**ivorce Coaching is a flexible, goal-oriented process designed to support, motivate, and guide people going through divorce to help them make the best possible decisions for their future, based on their particular interests, needs, and concerns. Divorce Coaches have different professional backgrounds and are selected based on the specific needs of the clients. For example, some Divorce Coaches are financial planners, mental health professionals, lawyers, or mediators who have experience dealing with divorcing clients."*

---

* (American Bar Association - Dispute Resolution Process, 2013)

Asking for help is a sign of strength and resourcefulness. Step into your power and greatness!

CHAPTER 2

What is a Divorce Coach?

In 2013, the American Bar Association added Divorce Coaching to a list of recognized alternative dispute resolution methods. Since then, the Divorce Coaching profession has been described as the fourth element of the divorce process. A Divorce Coach will work alongside the other professional members of a client's team to help the individual attain the best possible outcome in a dissolution of marriage. At this stage, many clients experience a gap between where they are and where they want to be. With the guidance of a Divorce Coach, clients will develop a roadmap for their divorce, gain help organizing the process, and learn skills necessary to communicate their needs, wants, and desires effectively without all of the emotional turmoil. Refocusing energy away from high conflict towards clarity and compromise is the goal.

Getting divorced is a time-consuming and challenging process. When individuals are in turmoil and get caught up in the emotional rollercoaster, they have difficulty accessing their logic and problem-solving abilities. Being overwhelmed leads to costly emotional and financial mistakes in divorce, which have long-term consequences for all parties involved. Divorce Coaches help clients become aware of how their mindset creates obstacles and how they have the power of choice to break down challenges. They guide their clients in a forward-focused path, encouraging them to honor their truth through self-discovery and help them make the best possible decisions for themselves. Divorce Coaches prepare clients, one forward step at a time, to turn the emotional side of divorce into the business of divorce, which ends up saving the client money and mental strife throughout the process. They assist in building up their client's resiliency to turbulence and in negotiating for their future by implementing conscious thought and intentional decision-making.

Divorce Coaching clients can find inner peace amongst the chaos. They are the expert in their lives and are guided to understand that no matter how stuck they feel, choices always exist. Divorce Coaches are the client's thinking partners; they create an environment of trust and safety where the individuals learn to move through the divorce process with pride and dignity while preserving self-esteem. The objective is to help clients show up as their best selves, navigate efficiently through the process, gain insight, and create a life vision for themselves based on specific plans for the future. Clients will gain an objective expert and sounding board in their corner to demistify the big "D" and guide them to become forward-focused, confident, courageous, and self-reliant.

Let your intelligence overpower your emotions. Consult and check-in with yourself daily!

CHAPTER 3

What Are the Benefits of Working with a Divorce Coach?

The Partnership <u>Creates a Nonjudgmental Collaboration:</u>

1. A client will work with an unbiased advocate and experienced coach who is the client's voice of reason and who fosters resiliency through self-discovery.
2. A client will acquire a professional to assist them in managing the divorce process and supporting them through challenging events.
3. A client will gain a sounding board and thinking partner.
4. A client will not feel alone and will have someone on their side with whom they can brainstorm ideas. The coach will be there to celebrate the client's successes and capabilities for future growth.
5. The coach will assist in educating the client about the process of divorce and how to create a strong team of professionals.

The Partnership Enhances Organizational Skills:

1. A coach will focus on a forward, goal-oriented, step-by-step process for each client.
2. A coach will guide the client as they sort through and organize their thoughts and paperwork.
3. A coach will help the client clarify what is important in divorce and assist them in understanding and avoiding the common pitfalls of the process.
4. A coach will encourage the client to define and redefine their personal goals and will devise a strategy to empower them to fulfill their desires.

The Partnership Provides Emotional Support:

1. A coach will prepare the client mentally for the rollercoaster of emotions that likely will be experienced.
2. A coach will help the client develop a sense of control during a challenging time.
3. A coach will create a safe, calm, and grounding place for the client during a difficult period when things seem uncertain.
4. A coach will help the client focus on thinking about how to overcome the challenge rather than dwelling on the challenge itself which enhances meaningful problem-solving.
5. A coach will encourage a client to break free from their feelings of victimhood and to show up as their best self.
6. A coach will build up strength in the client to move forward and take action.
7. A coach will teach the client skills to manage their emotions and responses.

What Are the Benefits of Working with a Divorce Coach?

The Partnership Improves Communication Skills:

1. A client will learn to make and express more informed and less reactive decisions.
2. A coach will help to create a credible and efficient client who is a more effective communicator so they can be heard and be a full participant in their divorce process.
3. A coach will assist in lowering the cost of attorney fees because the coach will help the client move beyond the story and will prepare the client for the business of divorce.

You are in control of your destiny. Tap into your power and advocate strongly for yourself!

CHAPTER 4

Why Hire a Divorce Coach if You Have a Family Law Attorney?

Divorce attorneys frequently find that their clients need professional guidance that extends beyond their legal realm. This is where a Divorce Coach can be a critical member of your team. Without someone there to remain steady, unbiased, and logical throughout the process, you may find yourself making grave mistakes. Divorce Coaches usually work alongside attorneys to help clients sift through what is important to them in divorce. The attorney you hire will be your guide through the legal process of the dissolution of your marriage. Most lawyers charge by the hour for any work they do for you, so you want to make the best use of their time. Divorce Coaches help you to be efficient and move beyond your story so that you can focus on the business of divorce.

A Divorce Coach will be your sounding board and thinking partner. Through internal guided work, meaningful discussion, and exercises, you will be encouraged to be proactive in establishing your goals and developing a strategic plan to move forward. You will have an experienced partner who specializes in the divorce process. The coach will help you frame your mindset to overcome obstacles and to manage your decisions with clarity so you are in a position to communicate more effectively. These actions will allow you to be in charge of your process, and they will make the time spent with your attorney more productive and significantly less costly.

*Life is not happening
in the past. Be
mindful of the
present and go for
what you desire!*

CHAPTER 5

What is the Difference between a Divorce Coach and a Therapist?

Many individuals contemplating divorce feel overburdened and stuck. During this time of transition, it is beneficial to have professional help supporting you through the dissolution of your marriage. There is confusion about Divorce Coaching and how it differs from therapy.

It is a therapist's job to help people identify and resolve difficulties stemming from their past. Therapists use a process-oriented approach to help identify patterns of thought and behavior that hold individuals back. They encourage people to work towards emotional resolutions to past problems. The main focus is on feelings within a framework of psychological and emotional issues. Therapy assumes patients need healing and seeks to provide a path. It helps to identify the personal challenges people are feeling as a result of divorce and will help to explore which past experiences created these issues.

The goal of a Divorce Coach is to walk clients through the practicalities of divorce and propel them into the next steps necessary to move in the direction of their desired outcomes. Coaching is goal-oriented and future-focused. The focal point is on present actions and desires. The process seeks to identify needs and interests in relation to how to move forward while building on client strengths.

Divorce Coaches are trained to understand the business and emotional side of divorce and how to educate their clients to be aware of what to expect along the way. The goal is to guide clients through the practical steps of the dissolution of a marriage efficiently and with the least amount of emotional interference in their decision-making.

Encourage yourself to find your voice. Focus on constant growth and development!

CHAPTER 6

Questions to Ask a Potential Divorce Coach

Background:

1. How long have you been practicing?
2. What certifications do you have?
3. What brought you into this line of work?
4. What do you enjoy the most about the profession?
5. What is your least favorite aspect of coaching?

Process:

1. Why is it important to hire a Divorce Coach?
2. Can you describe the typical client that comes to see you?
3. What are the biggest challenges many of your clients face?
4. Can you walk me through your process?
5. What should I expect during our first session?
6. Do you offer a complimentary session?
7. Do you give homework?
8. Will you help me organize all of my paperwork?
9. Will you attend professional meetings with me?
10. What is the average length of time you see clients?
11. How often do you meet with clients — weekly or monthly?
12. What helps you determine if a client is a good fit?

13. Do you meet in person, talk over the phone, or use video conferencing?
14. Do you offer packages or are you paid by the session?
15. What is your fee?
16. How do you work with the other professionals on my divorce team?

Personality:

1. How do you think your clients would describe you?
2. Who is your ideal client?
3. Are there certain clients you won't work with?

Your wisdom and insight will assist you in making sound choices. Cultivate what you want to bring into fruition!

CHAPTER 7

The Most Common Mistakes to Avoid in Divorce

Divorce is one of the most stressful and life-changing events. It not only impacts the microcosm of your family; it also affects your friends, coworkers, and your day-to-day routine as you transition from married life to a new way of living as a single person. The process is often frustrating, overwhelming, and difficult. It is imperative that you avoid common mistakes that others before you made that led to regret, despair, financial ruin, co-parenting issues, and an overall unfavorable outcome.

12 mistakes to avoid:

1. Not understanding your legal rights.
2. Not getting the right professional help.
3. Not thinking through and considering the pros and cons of your decisions.
4. Making decisions based on short-term emotional gain.
5. Giving away your power.
6. Wanting certainty and a guarantee for everything.
7. Being completely position-based by taking the "My way or the highway" approach.
8. Giving up on the process too soon by just wanting to get it over with.

9. Using your attorney as a therapist or Divorce Coach.
10. Remaining stuck with fear and grief.
11. Criticizing the other parent and negatively affecting your children's wellbeing.
12. Quickly moving on to another relationship and losing sight of negotiating for what you deserve.

A Divorce Coach will keep you cognizant of the pitfalls of the process throughout the dissolution of your marriage. You will be provided with the necessary support and tools to help you navigate all of the details so you feel confident and secure.

Choose your steps carefully. Acknowledge your efforts and honor your progress!

CHAPTER 8

States of Mind During the Divorce Process

There are different states of mind that individuals experience during the divorce process. As a result, many people often make shortsighted choices based on emotional reactions that don't take into account long-term best interests. A Divorce Coach can help you identify emotions that are extremely daunting so that you can focus intently on making sound decisions throughout the process.

The Rollercoaster:

Divorce is one of the most intense emotional experiences you will ever go through. The process is complicated, painful, exhausting, and life-changing. The dissolution of a marriage is a chaotic period of adjustment and redefinition. The emotions and thoughts attributed to the divorce process tend to create more psychological instability. Your life can feel like it is spiraling out of control and it becomes easy to wonder if things will ever improve. It is important to begin to practice a belief that emotions and thoughts are not fixed and uncontrollable. They come and go. No emotion is off limits while going through the divorce process. **Feelings are a guide — not your identity.** The path out of the emotional rollercoaster is acknowledging you don't have to live as a hostage of your emotional pain. It will pass. The key is to learn how to tune into your feelings. Self-awareness is your best friend. The more you learn about what upsets you, the better prepared you are to deal with it, and the easier it will be to make the necessary changes in order to move forward. Submit to the process and trust yourself. The more aware you become of the role you play in your own life, the more apt you will be to create a positive momentum that will push you forward. Learn to recognize what is not working for you. Letting go of the negative emotions that accompany the divorce process is hard and necessary in order to move on.

A Divorce Coach will partner with and guide you in developing a foundation of acceptance, accountability, compassion, choice, and the creation of the next chapter in your life.

Overwhelm:

For many people, divorce is a time of tremendous stress, disruption, resentment, chaos, uncertainty, shame, and self-doubt. Coming face-to-face with all of the different ways divorce disrupts your life is a lot to take in. It can feel like you are drowning in a sea of never-ending challenges and responsibilities. The process itself can be filled by emotional highs and lows. Many are overcome with paralyzing despair and feel stuck. When people become angry and emotional, the part of their brain that is associated with being reasonable and communicating effectively shuts down. When this happens, people do not realize that their abilities to process and make clear-headed decisions become hindered. Their judgment and ability to problem solve are negatively affected. The path back to emotional stability isn't instantaneous. There are so many life decisions to be made that many lose track of what is really important.

A Divorce Coach will be your partner in the process and will guide you in developing productive strategies, options, and insight.

Fear:

If your fear of divorce is paralyzing you, you are not alone. It doesn't matter who initiates the process. There are no guarantees and not knowing what the future will bring can make the present moment very scary. Divorce impacts life in a myriad of ways. The ambiguity, challenges, and responsibilities can make you feel like your life is falling apart. It is a horrible feeling and often leads to indecision. However, living in an unhealthy marriage doesn't feel amazing either. If you find yourself at a crossroads between your unhealthy marriage and your fear of divorce, the question becomes, **"Do you want to save your soul or your marriage?"** Being afraid of divorce is a very real fear. Denying it or pretending it doesn't exist won't make it go away. **Whatever you resist, will persist**. There is a "You" without your spouse. To find yourself, it is necessary to step through the fear and out of your comfort zone.

*A Divorce Coach will guide you in an effective way to manage your fears of divorce. You will learn skills to **Feel Everything And Rise (F.E.A.R.)**. You will be shown how to demystify the process and gain clarity as to what you could be facing. The more comfortable you feel, the greater ability you have to achieve your goals.*

Anger:

Feeling angry is normal and expected when going through the emotional turmoil of divorce. Anger is a very natural part of the process of moving forward. You may experience anger directed in a variety of ways depending on the situation that led to the divorce. If used in a healthy way, the emotion can be constructive. It can help you to break the bonds of affection and attachment towards your spouse and can propel you to begin taking control of your life. Anger can also help you get through the first and most painful stage of divorce by providing an outlet for inexpressible emotions. It is advisable to let out the anger in constructive and non-aggressive ways. If misused, anger can become self-defeating and self-destructive. The emotion can also cause mistakes in judgment that work against your best interests. Your feelings of anger will come and go. The emotion will drain so much of your energy that could be used for more productive things. **Anger is not a solution and does not solve anything.**

A Divorce Coach will help you identify triggers that cause you to feel angry and will support and empower you to overcome the emotional barriers that may be buried or not fully acknowledged. When you can release the negative feelings, you can begin to heal and move forward.

Loneliness:

The dissolution of your marriage can be lonely, isolating, and scary. Loneliness hurts and requires soothing. It is okay to have these feelings when the spouse you shared your life with is no longer part of your daily routine. The healthiest way through this emotion is to acknowledge and accept the fact that loneliness is a natural part of the divorce process. It is important to recognize that you can end your loneliness. Begin by feeling a sense of belonging to yourself. It is possible to achieve feeling complete, whole, and cared for by nurturing a relationship with yourself. **Being alone is a situation and does not mean being lonely.** This conscious mindset presents a space for you to heal and start over on your own terms. During this period, aim to show kindness to yourself and to be proactive about taking your life back. Allowing yourself time to breathe will create an opportunity for you to discover what brings out the best in you and what makes you happy. Being open to all the wonderful things your life has to offer and acknowledging your chance to explore them is the antidote to loneliness.

A Divorce Coach will assist you in acquiring the skills necessary to feel comfortable being alone during the divorce process. This empowering period of discovery will foster reflection, peace, self-confidence, and inner strength.

Sadness:

Deep sadness over the loss of your marriage is a common emotion. Whether your divorce came as a surprise or it was expected, feelings of pain are common. You may feel like you have no control over your life and that you are a victim. It is an unsettling time. Your marriage is over, routines are disrupted, the stress of transition exists, and there are legal and financial issues to be addressed. The sadness may seem insurmountable, and a void within your soul may exist. Unfortunately, your life doesn't stop just because you are hurting. **It is essential to remember that sadness isn't permanent.** Setting the intention and working hard to have a positive attitude is an important part of the emotional coping process. Moving forward must be your main goal. Remind yourself that **you are worthy of all good things** and that you deserve to be happy. Within time, your sadness will begin to lift, and you will find yourself moving on.

A Divorce Coach will partner with you to overcome the emotional crisis you are in. You will explore new possibilities and participate in life-changing exercises. There is a silver lining to all your sadness. You will gain wisdom, courage, and strength from having gone through this challenging experience.

Guilt:

Many people carry a sense of personal failure when getting divorced and internalize a sense of shame or inadequacy that is misplaced and unhelpful. Guilt, shame, and regret are common emotions experienced at the end of a marriage. If you are like most people, you took your marriage vows seriously. You believed you would be married forever. As time passed, things changed. Allowing feelings of guilt, shame, or regret to occupy space in your brain decreases your self-worth and energy. These feelings have the tendency to entrap you, which limit your ability to function in a healthy way and keep you from moving forward. **Guilt is not the truth. It is just a feeling.** Getting divorced is not necessarily bad, good, right, or wrong. The process is whatever you make it. **You are much more than your divorce!**

A Divorce Coach will be the objective listener who will support you in breaking free from the sense of guilt, shame, or regret that imprisons your mind. Having an objective listener on your side can be the difference between stagnation and personal growth.

Grief:

Being distressed when a marriage ends is normal. Getting a divorce marks the beginning of enormous change in your life. It is natural to grieve for the loss of a relationship you expected to last, and for a future you had planned but will now be altered. Like any kind of loss, divorce may trigger a variety of reactions.

Many people experience five distinct stages of grief including **denial, bargaining, depression, anger**, and finally **acceptance**. People go through these stages in various orders and for different periods of time. It is critical to acknowledge that the grief and recovery process does have a beginning, middle, and end. Understanding these stages is helpful when it comes to talking about divorce and decision-making. Identifying the stage of grief you are experiencing and being aware of it is an important step towards ensuring that you will make the best choices during your divorce process.

While you are attempting to manage your emotional recovery during your divorce journey, plan on being gentle with yourself, seek support, and allow yourself to feel the range of emotions as they come.

A Divorce Coach will guide you to discover what you can do to steadily overcome your grief, to avoid shortsighted decisions, and to move forward in a positive, productive, and healthy manner.

How you react and respond to a situation impacts the outcome. Use your power of choice!

CHAPTER 9

Paths You Might Experience During the Dissolution of Your Marriage

Denial:

Denial is an emotional buffer that many individuals experience during and at the end of a marriage. It is a natural defense mechanism your psyche uses to protect you from becoming emotionally overburdened. Denial is usually the first reaction individuals have when divorce is discussed. Everything can feel surreal and hard to accept during this time. There is a certain numbness, disbelief, and emotional shock that occurs. It is normal to convince yourself that the thought of divorce is temporary; your partner is still in love with you; your spouse will come back to you in the end; your children will keep you together, and the spark in your marriage can be reignited. It is common during this period for individuals to go on with daily life as if nothing major is happening and to avoid talking to close friends and family about the impending divorce. Many want to escape the reality and the emotional pain by not acknowledging the actuality of the divorce. It is important to remember that **denial is temporary.** Pushing yourself to face the reality of your divorce will help you tremendously.

A Divorce Coach will partner with you to acquire skills necessary to avoid emotionally driven decisions which are usually not sound ones. You will also be assisted in developing goals for redefining your life during this major transition.

Bargaining:

It can be painful and frightening to accept the reality of divorce. Many wish to turn back time or decide to do whatever they can to keep the marriage from ending. Bargaining occurs when an individual anticipates a great loss. It is a common desperate measure usually aimed to keep the marriage intact and to minimize the possibility of divorce from happening. Bargaining can also occur through replaying everything that went wrong in the marriage and letting one's mind overthink different "What if?" questions and scenarios.

There are many reasons why a person bargains during the demise of a marriage. Aside from wanting to keep the long-term relationship together, some want to avoid the loneliness and sadness that comes with divorce. Others want to circumvent all of the gossip and stigma that goes along with the end of a marriage. Additionally, individuals bargain to preserve the family unit because of the children and the desire to avoid going through the overwhelming legal, financial, and emotional aspects of divorce.

During the bargaining stage, people often allow their fears of the unknown to override the reality that ending the marriage could be the healthiest solution for both parties. It is important to recognize that getting to the bargaining stage makes you closer to accepting the dissolution of your marriage. **With endings, comes the possibility of beautiful beginnings.**

A Divorce Coach will assist you in exploring the reasons why your relationship did not work so that you are clear about what you desire moving forward. Recognizing and owning your contribution to the end of your marriage will create the momentum you need to start the next chapter of your life.

Courage:

When your marriage is coming to an end, you are at a crossroad in your life and there are no guarantees. It is normal to feel lost, confused, and alone. Give yourself time. It takes a lot of soul-searching and introspection to become clear about what you really want to manifest in your life moving forward. Allow yourself to dream. Be kind and gentle with yourself. Know that anxiety and fear are a natural part of the human experience. **It is important to recognize that good things often come from reaching out into the unknown.** You have control over every decision you make.

A Divorce Coach will guide you to develop an action plan that will strengthen your resolve and lead you forward. The partnership will provide you with tools to help you to grow in your own truth.

Choice:

The process of divorce requires making decisions and accepting the inevitability of change. People experience a variety of emotions during this time and often feel like their lives are out of control. **Your power to choose always**

exists. You can become the creator of your desires. You are never really stuck. All crossroads require you to ask yourself whether you are a victim of your situation or a creator of your future. Choice is an option you have every single time something happens in your life. It is important that you make decisions that support your goals, happiness, and well-being. Only you have the power to choose what serves you and what defeats you. The right to react in a less emotionally disruptive way is up to you.

A Divorce Coach will teach you skills to enhance your ability to exercise your power of choice. You will develop tools to control your thoughts and actions to show up as your best self, someone who is always evolving, growing, and learning. You will discover who you are so you can develop confidence and trust in yourself.

Clarity:

Many people live in a cycle of decision and indecision before they get the clarity that is needed to step toward what they want. People often deny, minimize, or rationalize the reasons for the end of their marriage. It is important to understand that everyone who goes through divorce is vulnerable and conflicted in some way. Recognizing the conflict and owning that there are different parts you will be struggling with at various times, is part of the process. There are many important decisions to be made, and it is challenging to problem-solve and think clearly while inundated with emotions. Taking a step back in the process and looking at the situation from a distance has proven to be extremely effective. **Clarity requires you to be objective and detached enough to see reality as it is without judgment.** Fostering your truth will make it easier to take effective action.

A Divorce Coach will assist you in gaining the clarity and confidence needed for you to negotiate for your future from a position of strength, understanding, and respect.

Hope:

Life does not end after divorce. It is a very hard time and marks the end of your marriage, but the experience does not have to prevent you from dreaming again. The change is an opportunity to create new possibilities. You have the power to move forward toward a more fulfilling life. Allow yourself to honestly face where you are at the present moment and begin to accept your new role as a single person. Know that having hope about the possibilities to come and honestly facing your vulnerabilities will help you to start healing and moving into the next chapter of your life. This is a precious time and an opportunity to rediscover who you are and what makes you happy. Remember that the pain will not last forever. It will pass. Be kind to yourself and empower your soul to take small steps towards positive change. Value yourself and all that you have to contribute. Finding hope is how you'll make it through the most painful part of your divorce journey and move on to happiness again.

A Divorce Coach will partner with you to develop the fortitude and skills needed for you to embrace your new chapter with positive energy and hope for all that is possible.

Acceptance:

Accepting your divorce is a matter of choice and a critical component to your recovery. It doesn't mean that you like it or that it is fair. The only thing you have control over is how you choose to see things and how you react to the curveballs that life delivers. **Mourning the loss of your marriage is natural**. It is challenging to move past the pain of divorce and to begin to rebuild a life you never intended to live. Not accepting your divorce as a reality keeps you stuck in the past and doesn't change anything. It is very difficult to live a productive life in the present moment and plan for the future if your head and heart are focused on what used to be. It is about self-worth. **Perspective is everything.** Learning to accept the reality of your divorce and to consciously focus on your blessings will help you develop the clarity you need to begin to live your life to the fullest.

Changing is a matter of conscious choice, desire, effort, and commitment to oneself. The truth is that you have two choices: **You can remain stuck in your pain or you can do the challenging work that it takes to move forward.** There are four steps in learning how to come to terms with your divorce:

1. Accept where you are right now.
2. Take responsibility for your actions and own your own mistakes.
3. Practice mindfulness and gratitude.
4. Take advantage of the opportunity for a new beginning.

Through these steps you will learn to let go of the negative emotions of anger, blame, resentment, and regret. This practice will allow you the freedom to move forward in creating a life based on your curiosities and values.

A Divorce Coach will guide you through self-help activities and will teach you skills to overcome obstacles so that you feel empowered to move through your divorce.

Embracing the Single Life:

After divorce, it can feel like you have been stripped of your identity and the world, as you know it. **The dissolution of your marriage is not the end of your life. It is just a detour.** When you have mourned and grieved properly for the end of your marriage, letting go and moving on will become more bearable and realistic. Your new status will feel like the natural way to move forward, and you will begin to embrace your life as a single person. This stage will be the beginning of a new journey towards finding personal fulfillment and happiness. Take this time as an opportunity to learn valuable lessons and to improve yourself. Nurture what you are grateful for, give time to your children and other loved ones, reconnect with family and friends, explore new possibilities, and reinvest in yourself.

A Divorce Coach will support you through the transition of being married to being single. You will be guided to explore many different paths so that you can create a life for yourself that is fulfilling.

Every setback leaves the door open for a breakthrough. Walk forward and open your heart to change!

Section 2

The Elements of Divorce

DIVORCE CHECKLIST
Understanding the four stages of divorce:

1. Deliberation:

Contemplating your divorce and how best to organize for the process.

2. Preparation:

Getting ready emotionally and financially to end your marriage.

3. Separation:

Deciding on the best legal process for the dissolution of your marriage and obtaining all the legal documents needed.

4. Manifestation:

Spending time thinking about what you want moving forward and putting a plan of action in place.

*Strive to be a warrior
not a worrier.
You are resilient!*

CHAPTER 10

Where Do I Begin?

For many individuals, the divorce process is unfamiliar and scary. It is a critical turning point. Knowing where and how to start can make all the difference. If you are contemplating divorce, now is the time to start doing your research and to develop a plan of action so that you can make informed decisions. It is important to understand the framework of the process and how to move through it in a productive manner. ***Planning is key!***

Divorce is not a one-size-fits-all approach - every divorce is different. A constructive place to begin learning about how to navigate the divorce process is by following Ilyssa Panitz, a divorce journalist, Host of "The Divorce Hour with Ilyssa Panitz" on CRN Digital Talk Radio, and the Director of Content for the National Association of Divorce Professionals. She provides insightful material on the divorce process. Ilyssa writes a weekly column for *Authority Magazine* entitled, "5 Things You Need to Know to Survive and Thrive During and After Divorce." Her writing is devoted to sharing educational and empowering interview-oriented articles featuring professionals in the divorce industry. Ilyssa's pieces and radio show offer individuals contemplating or going through the divorce process with valuable resources and information to move them forward. (medium.com/@ilyssapanitz)

It is also helpful to understand that at the heart of every divorce there are four issues:

1. Division of community and/or marital property
2. Division of debt
3. Custody of any children
4. Payment of child and/or spousal support/ professional fees

Compartmentalizing the issues in the divorce process into four categories makes the process more manageable:

1. Emotional Piece
2. Organizational Piece
3. Legal Piece
4. Financial Piece

Going through a divorce is multidimensional. Legal expertise alone is insufficient for individuals to achieve a successful dissolution of marriage. Lawyers are trained as courtroom advocates and negotiators, but they are not necessarily experts in how to best organize for the process, how to move through the emotional challenges, or how to best plan financially. It is important to put some thought into building, *"Team You."* Each divorce professional brings a specific strength to your side and works together to help you get the best outcome for your future. You want to make sure you feel heard, seen, and cared for.

Whether your divorce issues are simple or complex, you will be asked to produce many documents. Gathering the information in an organized manner will make the entire divorce process less burdensome on you in the present moment and will help you achieve the best possible results in the long run. The checklists on the following pages lay out much of what you will need to prepare and think about for the dissolution of your marriage.

Be in the here and now. Motivate yourself to become better not bitter!

CHAPTER 11

Emotional Piece

As you initially think about ending your marriage, you may or may not know if you want a divorce. This feeling is completely normal. What you want might be entirely different from what you ultimately decide you have to do. Your job, in the present moment, is to learn about what is possible for you and your family. **The intention you bring to this process is crucial.** The more prepared you are, the greater chance your nervous system will feel calmer and more regulated. Planning will foster less reactivity and more proactive, knowledge-based decision making as it relates to the legal process, life restructuring, and relationship renegotiation necessary for moving forward.

Initial steps:

○ Reflect on how you want to be **perceived** and then use that to keep your emotions in control.

○ Be **kind to yourself**. Understand that there will be times you feel extremely emotional.

○ A productive first step is to contact a compassionate professional such as a **Divorce Coach** who can help you understand the legal, financial, and emotional process you may be facing and the issues that are holding you back from making a decision. Being more educated about the divorce process when you consult with lawyers, financial advisors, or mediators will make your time with them more productive and should save you money.

○ If you feel you may be a **victim of abuse**, take action and get assistance immediately.

○ Create a **potential plan** regarding how you are going to tell your spouse (if you are the one asking for a divorce), and your loved ones. Proactively thinking about a strategy will save you many headaches down the road.

○ **Be careful in whom you confide. This statement includes family.** Few people can be truly objective, and fewer still are marriage or divorce experts. Yet, there will be many opinions and judgements from people around you. Lean on individuals who you trust and who support you in a non-judgmental way.

○ **If the decision is divorce**, think of how your kids are being impacted now and long term, and plan accordingly.

○ Once your divorce process is public knowledge, it is useful to have an explanation that you feel comfortable sharing with others. An **elevator speech** is a brief statement that communicates what you want to say about the dissolution of your marriage in about 20-30 seconds. The benefit of having an elevator speech prepared during this emotional period of your life is to be proactive in your communication while at the same time limiting awkward conversations that deplete your energy. **Be mindful that individuals treat you the way you allow them to.** It is essential to practice your personal boundaries at this time. Share only what you deem necessary.

○ Get clear on what negative **triggers** you experience, as they relate to your soon to be ex-spouse. Coming up with rooted and centered responses when you start to feel your buttons being pushed is a very healthy and proactive strategy, and it will assist you in being less reactive. **The game plan is your lifeline**, and it will reduce the chances of high conflict. When you are better able to manage the emotional impact, you will be more productive and solution-oriented. There are 5 categories of triggers to be aware of that upset individuals when they feel threatened:

Sense of *status*:	Competency as an adult or parent
Sense of *certainty*:	Ability to rely on the other person as it relates to behavior and reliability
Sense of *autonomy*:	Ability to act on your own values and interests without someone getting in your way
Sense of *relatedness*:	Feeling of belonging to the family or group
Sense of *fairness*:	Feeling that you receive impartial treatment

○ Decide on a **media game plan:**

1. **Change your passwords and security questions for account recovery.** Make sure your spouse won't be able to guess the answers to those questions.

2. **Open a new email account.** Use this new address to conduct your personal business from this point forward and to sign up for divorce information and

newsletters that might guide your thinking and understanding.

3. **Restrict your online activity.** Some divorcing individuals deactivate their social media accounts while their marriage is in turmoil, then reactivate them when the dust settles after the divorce. Others simply post less often than they used to, and only in the blandest, most unassailable fashion. Take whatever steps are sensible for you to prevent online mishaps while you are divorcing. Never post about a new relationship, and never post in a way that might even suggest you are spending money frivolously. Attorneys can use "electronic discovery" to access information from your social media sites.

4. **Review and tighten privacy settings on social media accounts.** Remember, if your social media contacts do not share your concerns, you are still vulnerable to a negative outcome in ways you cannot control.

5. **Keep control of your devices.** Many of us share calendars and other apps across more than one device and sync them automatically. While it can be convenient for keeping the whole family up to date, this can also mean that your text messages and other communications are not as private as you need them to be. You might also want to turn off location tracking on your devices.

○ **"No" is a complete answer.** During this period, many people, with good intentions, will reach out to you and invite you to dinners, parties, and other activities. **Listen to your internal dialogue**. If you are not up to attending, thank them for the invitation and politely tell them that you are unable to make it this time but would love to be invited again in the near future. During the divorce process, it is essential to take care of yourself and honor what genuinely feels good.

○ **Know that there is life after divorce.** If the dissolution of your marriage is the answer, the checklists on the following pages will help guide you. What stands directly in front of you is moving through the divorce process and ensuring your divorce recovery. **You WILL process and recover in your own way and at your own pace.**

○ **This is your journey.** You will be the one signing the divorce papers if that is the route you choose (not your attorney, accountant, Divorce Coach, therapist, financial advisor, friends, or parents). The settlement needs to suit you and your children, if you have any. **You have the right and the responsibility to drive the tone and pace of the process** with the guidance of the professionals on your team. You know your family dynamic better than anyone. Set the goal of staying in your power and making sure your voice is heard.

○ **Take the time to figure out what you want and need.** Do not let anyone dictate to you how you must live your life.

○ **Be proactive not reactive!**

Planning will lead you to increased productivity and a more fulfilled version of yourself. Begin by taking inventory of what you want to accomplish and then take action!

CHAPTER 12

Organizational Piece

Preparation is essential for your nervous system to feel calmer and more regulated during a dissolution of marriage. In order to make things less stressful and more manageable, set the intention of determining how you would like to organize yourself. Creating one system of note taking and filing will make things easier to navigate during the divorce process. You can use a binder system with hard copies of everything, create your own digital folder, or subscribe to a digitally-secured platform. Whatever system you choose, it must be kept in a safe place or password protected, where only you can access it or find it.

Initial steps:

o It is essential to remember the **6 P's in the divorce process**:

1. **Proper**
2. **Planning**
3. **Prevents**
4. **Poor**
5. **Performance** (and)
6. **Pitfalls**

o **Items to purchase for a binder system:**

1. 6" binder (for copies of all documents and correspondence). It must be kept in a safe place at all times.

2. At-A-Glance Notetaker Monthly Planner 9" X 11" to be kept in the binder or clipped to it.

3. Three packages of 8 Bag Tab Insertable Dividers:

Make the following tabs for the dividers:

a. Copies of correspondence with **attorney**

b. Copies of legal documents

c. Time Log: Write the date, a description of the subject matter, and then keep track of the length of time that elapses regarding emails, calls, or meetings with attorney. (You want to be able to review your bills to check for accuracy.)

d. Copies of correspondence with an **accountant**

e. Copies of financial documents

f. Time Log: Write the date, a description of the subject matter, and then keep track of the length of time that elapses regarding emails, calls, or meetings with financial professional. (You want to be able to review your bills to check for accuracy.)

g. Copies of correspondence with a **financial advisor**

h. Copies of financial documents

i. Time Log: Write the date, a description of the subject matter, and then keep track of the length of time that elapses regarding emails, calls, or meetings with financial professional. (You want to be able to review your bills to check for accuracy.)

j. Copies of correspondence with an **estate lawyer**

k. Copies of legal documents

l. Time Log: Write the date, a description of the subject matter, and then keep track of the length of time that elapses regarding emails, calls, or meetings with attorney. (You want to be able to review your bills to check for accuracy.)

    m. Copies of personal documents
    n. Parenting Issues
    o. Notes from **Coaching** Sessions
    p. Notes from **Therapy** Sessions
    q. Personal Information
    r. Journal

4. College Ruled Paper: (One system of notetaking and filing makes the process more fluid and efficient.)
5. Three-hole punch
6. Stapler
7. Download a scanner app like Turbo Scan. (You will be scanning several documents to your divorce professionals.)

○ **Items to purchase for your own digital system:**

1. A digital device where you can securely create and upload the same tabs as for the binder system above.

○ **Items to purchase for a digitally-secure platform:**

1. A platform subscription that can digitally manage your divorce data.

    Dtour.life (https://www.dtour.life) is an online platform to consider. It is designed to fully address the most challenging pain points in the divorce process. The platform provides:

    a. Divorcing spouses with education and robust financial and parenting tools to effectively address the day-to-day workflow required by the process. The result is a significant improvement in time management, cost savings, and a greater sense of personal empowerment.

b. A digital experience so that data can be easily collected and updated by the client and divorce professionals along the way and accessed throughout the entire process for on-going discussions.

c. A visual experience so that everyone on the team can make sense of the details as well as understand the nature of the assets and debts and financial inflows and outflows.

d. A digital collaboration with the most advanced security and encryption technology available so that all members of the team have access to real-time data and documents while using a platform that is extremely user-friendly.

e. Day-to-day one-click access for divorce professionals that facilitates the gathering, organization, and analysis of all case data to significantly streamline the process. It also enables them to assess the venue, strategize, file, and develop clear financial settlement scenarios and discussions while using sophisticated tools.

o **Contact information**: List all of your email accounts and other contact information, your emergency contacts, your employer, and anyone with duties or powers under any of the other documents

o List of all your **social media accounts** and information on how to gain access (password) and/or otherwise deal with those accounts. It is essential that this information be kept confidential; however, it is okay to give access to a trusted person, just in case.

o   Make a copy of your updated **resumé.** You will want your most updated resumé with these documents because it will have information about your current and last employer, any professional associations and organizations to which you belong, any schools you attended, and degrees/certifications you have.

o   **List of names, addresses, and phone numbers of close friends and relatives, and all doctors, lawyers, therapists, coaches, and financial accountants/ advisors that make up your professional team.**

o   Many parents with young children purchase a **whiteboard calendar, eraser, and Expo markers** for timesharing and specific special events to keep in a visible area for their kids to be able to see and refer to. The calendar is helpful and reassuring for them. If children are too young to read, color coding mom and dad timesharing times and events is an alternative.

Communicate clearly and concisely. Own how your process unfolds!

CHAPTER 13

Legal Piece

The legal process can be very intimidating and confusing. It is up to you to decide the kind of divorce process that will work best for you. A family law attorney and/or a mediator will make sure that all of the steps and requirements of your state's laws are met to make the dissolution of your marriage legal. To begin the process, consider the following:

Initial Steps:

○ Ask your Divorce Coach, therapist, and friends for **vetted referrals** to divorce attorneys. Be mindful of a tactic called **"conflicting out"** potential divorce lawyers. This strategy is used by some soon to be ex-spouses to run to divorce attorneys and have initial consultations, thereby creating a conflict of interest. Once the conflict exists, the other spouse is no longer able to hire that lawyer because they are conflicted out. This is the general rule:

"Attorneys are required to maintain a conflict database. The conflict database is a list of people that the attorney has created attorney-client relationships with, and parties opposed to them. If someone from the other side of the case approaches the attorney, then the attorney searches the database and finds that person, thus preventing them from having privileged conversations with both parties and getting information in confidence that could be used against each side." **

** (Guys, n.d.)

Educate yourself about the laws in your state.

- ○ **Knowledge is key. Schedule consultations** with several attorneys and/or mediators to learn about and discuss the best divorce process for your case. Keep in mind that you are seeking perspective and feedback about your particular situation. You also want someone that you can trust and feel comfortable with. It is important to find a lawyer whose values align with yours. Additionally, you can also visit the attorney's website and research online what past clients have written. **Remember, you have choices**!

- ○ When you go to the **consultations**, bring specific questions and basic information about you and your family:

  -Spouses: Birthdates, occupation, employment history, annual income, date of marriage, whether you own or rent your home, etc.

  -Children: Birthdates, special needs, etc.

- ○ There are **several legal ways to end your marriage**. Take the time to learn and think about which resolution process is the best for you and your family. When researching your options, keep your goals in mind. Determining the aspects that are most important to you and your family in the short- and long-term will help guide your process decision.

Process Options:

1. ***Pro-Se:***

   Filing a Pro-Se divorce means that you are representing yourself rather than hiring an attorney for your divorce case. The entire process of getting a divorce is the same, but you are personally responsible for completing and filing the legal forms and attending any hearings.

2. ***Traditional Litigation:***

   Lawyers who practice in this area of the law focus on issues involving disputes in family relationships, such as divorce, child custody, or paternity. Traditional marital and family litigation requires the parties, with or without being represented by an attorney, to exchange documents and information. The goal is to negotiate a settlement out of court, which happens in the majority of divorce cases. Traditional marital and family litigation in court becomes necessary when one or both spouses refuse to turn over essential documentation, decline to participate, have high-conflict personalities, or otherwise attempt to hinder the process. If the issues cannot be resolved between the parties out of court, a trial date will be scheduled. After reviewing evidence and hearing oral arguments by the parties or the family law attorneys from both sides, at a court proceeding, the judge will issue a ruling. This type of litigation can be the most expensive and emotionally-draining way to get divorced. It is also important to keep in mind that filed documents can become part of the public record, which means that anyone can access the information.

3. *Collaborative Process:*

The Collaborative Process is a voluntary dispute resolution process in which parties maintain open communication and information sharing to negotiate a mutually acceptable settlement without having courts decide issues.

   a. The parties sign a collaborative participation agreement describing the nature and scope of the matter.
   b. The parties voluntarily disclose all information which is relevant and material to the matter that must be decided.
   c. The parties agree to use good faith efforts in their negotiations to reach a mutually acceptable settlement.
   d. Each party must be represented by a lawyer whose representation terminates upon the undertaking of any contested court proceeding.
   e. The parties may engage professionals in mental health, finance, and other areas as needed whose engagement terminates upon the undertaking of any contested court proceeding. ***

The team works toward reaching a settlement on fair and equitable terms without the financial and emotional cost that often accompanies litigation. It also empowers the respective parties to make their own decisions and customize the terms of an agreement based upon their particular needs and interests in an efficient, expeditious, and civil manner.

4. *Mediation:*

A procedure in which the parties discuss their disputes with the assistance of a **mediator** who is a trained

*** (IACP, International Academy Collaborative of Professionals)

impartial third party that will assist them in reaching a settlement.

5. *Arbitration:*

A private process where disputing parties agree that a neutral third party called an **arbitrator** has the authority to make a binding decision about the dispute after receiving evidence and hearing arguments instead of going to court. Some states prohibit the use of an arbitrator in matters involving children.

Other Items to Contemplate:

○ **Consider having a friend or a Divorce Coach accompany you to some or all of the professional meetings.** There is a lot to learn and keep track of, especially when you are feeling emotional and overwhelmed.

○ **Understand the legal issues and the choices you have surrounding the dissolution of your marriage.** The acronym, **P.E.A.C.E.**, represents the five key issues you must be aware of in the process because it helps to create a framework regarding the matters that come up with divorce:

(The National Law Review Volume X, 2020)

P: Parenting Plan:

The legal document that governs the parenting and timesharing agreement between the parents. The terms are typically negotiated by the parents, but if they cannot agree on how to parent their children, the judge can order them to comply with a parenting plan forced on them.

E: Equitable Distribution of Marital Assets and Liabilities:

A legal term used to describe the division of marital property and liabilities in most states. In theory, the marital assets and liabilities are distributed equitably between the parties. Assets and liabilities are considered as either non-marital (separate) or martial. The goal of equitable distribution is to consider the needs of each party and the facts of the case. It is determined on a case-by-case basis, is subject to negotiation between the two parties, and can end up at the discretion of the judge, if the case goes to trial.

A: Alimony:

Court ordered support payments agreed to by the parties or awarded to a spouse or former spouse by a judge. The purpose is to provide financial support to the spouse who makes a lower income, or in some cases, no income at all when the other spouse can afford to contribute funds to help support the less fortunate spouse. It is mostly based on need and ability to pay.

C: Child Support:

Money that one parent pays to the other parent when there is a disparity in earning capacity and possibly timesharing. The monetary payment serves as a parental contribution for the child's basic living expenses, such as food, clothing, shelter, transportation, and entertainment. The sum takes into account the income of both parents, certain deductions and expenses, and the number of over-nights the children spend with each parent.

E: Everything Else:

Every case has its own individual issues which need to be addressed and decided. Examples of some matters include such things as attorney fees, mental health, domestic violence, substance abuse, sharing costs of college education for a child, taking back a former name, allowing grandparents to have substantial time with the children, etc. ****

○ Always ask your attorney for your **options** regarding the legal process and know the **cost**. Remember that if you are going the traditional litigation route to get divorced, it is your right to tell your attorney not to file anything without speaking to you first.

○ Consider asking the professionals on your team to cc you and send you copies of all communications regarding your case. **You are in charge and have the right to know everything that is going on.**

○ **Store your legal documents in a safe place**. It may be helpful to open a safe deposit box in only your name. You can store original documents in the safe deposit box or at a family member's home. Additionally, make sure that you have a safe backup of the documents stored in your computer and that you frequently back it up. These documents will be very important for your attorney during your divorce.

○ **Start writing down challenging situations between you and your soon-to-be ex in the journal section of the binder or in the At-A-Glance Notetaker Monthly**

****   (Gisondo, 2020)

Planner. If your attorney ever has to draft a motion to tell the court your story, and to ask for relief from the judge, it can be tough to remember the details during such a stressful and emotional time. It will be helpful to have dated documentation.

○ Decide if you are going to **request a legal name change**.

Obtain Essential Personal Documents and Information:

○ **Social Security** card containing your full legal name

○ **Birth certificate(s) for you and your children**

○ **Passport(s) for you and your children**

○ **Driver's License**

○ **Marriage certificate**

○ **Separation agreement**

○ **Prenuptial or postnuptial agreement**

○ **Armed Forces discharge papers**

○ **Your soon-to-be ex's basic information:** full name, date of birth, and social security number.

○ **Contact information for your soon-to-be ex** such as an address, landline or cell phone number, and email address.

○ **Name and contact information for your soon-to-be ex's legal, financial, or mental health professional** if they have one.

Organize your estate documents

○ Contact an *estate attorney* to update your estate planning documents. An estate planning attorney is an experienced and licensed law professional with a thorough understanding of the state and federal laws that affect how your estate will be inventoried, valued, dispersed, and taxed after your death.

○ **Documents to consider creating or updating with an estate attorney:**

1. *Last Will and Testament:*

   An individual creates a will while still alive. A will indicates the manner in which the person wishes for their estate to be managed at the time of their death.

   You will not be able to completely remove your spouse from your will until your divorce is finalized unless there is a Postnuptial Agreement stating so. However, you may want to consider taking steps to remove them to the extent that your state allows and naming someone else to the extent that your state allows.

2. *Living Will:*

   A written, legal document that details the medical treatments you would and would not want to be used to keep you alive, as well as your preferences for other medical decisions such as pain management or organ donation.

   You may want to consider taking steps to remove your spouse and naming someone else to the extent that your state allows with respect to providing the medical treatments that you would or would not want if you became terminally ill or unable to make your own medical decisions.

3. ***Health Care Proxy:***

A legal document that allows you to choose someone you trust to make health care decisions on your behalf.

You may want to consider taking steps to remove your spouse of the responsibility of making medical decisions should you be unable to do so and naming someone else to the extent that your state allows.

4. ***Durable Power of Attorney:***

A legal document that gives another person the right to do certain things for the maker of the Durable Power of Attorney. What those things are depends upon what the document outlines. A person giving a Durable Power of Attorney can make it very broad or can limit it to certain acts.

You may want to consider taking steps to remove your spouse and name someone else to the extent that your state allows.

○ ***All of your beneficiary designations:***

In consultation with your estate planning and divorce attorneys, you may want to consider taking steps to remove your spouse as a beneficiary on financial related accounts and name someone else to the extent that your state allows.

○ ***Trusts:***

If there is a trust set up, at least be able to provide the documentation.

Issues Pertaining to the Children:

○ Keep a childcare diary **in the journal section of the binder or in the At-A-Glance Notetaker Monthly Planner.** If there's a dispute between you and your spouse with regard to taking care of the children, you will benefit by having kept a **detailed and dated record** of who does what with the kids. Write down who takes them to their appointments, meets with teachers and counselors, attends their extracurricular activities, etc.

○ **Consider how you are going to effectively correspond with your soon-to-be ex-spouse and parent to your children.** Co-parenting can often be less challenging for families when parents are able to communicate clearly and come to agreements on their own.

> The **OurFamilyWizard®** online platform (ourfamilywizard.com) offers co-parents practical tools for managing every aspect of their parenting plan while also limiting the potential for conflict. It is an app designed to facilitate effective communication between divorced or separated families. Features in the app help parents:
>
> 1. Handle day-to-day decisions on their own on matters like scheduling and expenses.
> 2. Document correspondence between one another. Every entry is dated and timestamped to prevent misunderstandings and to maintain a transparent record that parents can download as needed.
> 3. Keep their professional team updated with respect to co-parenting issues. The app allows practitioners to access messages and other activity between clients and their co-parents in

the platform whenever necessary which gives the professionals on the team the information they need to assist parents.

OurFamilyWizard® is committed to removing conflict and improving the lives of the children. Its intent is also to decrease the need for involvement with the courts, judges, attorneys, and other divorce professionals.

○ Getting divorced when there are children involved makes the process more complex and overwhelming. Finding helpful resources, advice, and tools you need to create the best possible outcome for you and your children is essential. Consider reading *How Do I Tell the Kids About the Divorce? A Create-a-Storybook Guide to Preparing Your Children -- With Love!* written by Rosalind Sedacca, CDC. She is recognized as The Voice of Child-Centered Divorce and the founder of the Child-Centered Divorce Network. Rosalind helps parents protect their children before, during, and long after divorce. To learn more about her services and to get her free eBook on co-parenting effectively, visit: childcentereddivorce.com.

Parenting Plan:

While it is impossible to include every issue that might arise regarding a child, the agreement is to ensure that there is little room for misunderstanding, misinterpretation, and that the contract can easily be enforced if the need arises. It is important to keep in mind that the most successful plans are the ones that put your child's needs first. Below are some specifics to consider including in your parenting agreement:

- Daily decision-making autonomy (bedtime, homework, diet, screen time, gaming, etc.)
- Discipline
- Medical decisions: joint or one spouse, specific doctors, specific treatments, vaccinations, etc.
- Therapy visits
- Orthodontist: braces, etc.
- Emergency notification policy
- Time sharing schedule/responsibilities including transportation related to child exchanges
- Mode and frequency of daily communication
- A First Right of Caretaking Clause
- Supervision: Can the child be left alone, for how long, and with who?
- As needed babysitting: Who is permitted or not permitted to watch the child?
- Nanny/Housekeeper: Background check, DMV report for hired help, confidentiality agreement, etc.
- Policy for cancelled time sharing
- Clothing & Possessions such as toys, electronics, books, etc. Agree upfront about how things will be purchased and if the items can freely travel with the child
- Travel & Vacation stipulations, logistics, and expenses
- Possession of travel documents such as passports, Global Entry, etc. when children are not traveling
- Time sharing and travel during national or state emergencies
- Future family events such as weddings, funerals, etc.
- Digital assets like family photos
- Gift giving responsibilities for birthdays, parties, special events, etc.
- Provision for contact or no contact with specific individuals

- Introduction of significant others to child (time period, overnights, etc.)
- How a child will address a new significant other
- Education decisions (Private/public, tuition, uniforms, etc.)
- Extracurricular activities
- Religious upbringing/religious school
- Special events/religious celebrations
- Tutoring: Core academics, SAT/ACT, Subject Area Tests, etc.
- Provision for limiting either parent's ability to make any major changes to the child's appearance without written consent of the other such as haircuts, hair coloring, ear piercing, tattoos, etc.
- Summer camp/programs
- Cell phone expenses
- Weekly/monthly allowance
- Trainer/coach for sports
- Music lessons (other lessons for special interests)
- Relocation provisions
- Taxes
- Provision for cord blood storage and frozen embryos
- Rental properties: Is a parent permitted to rent a portion of the home while the child is there?
- Provision to alternate tax credit/dependency deduction
- Independent College Advisor expenses
- College application expenses
- College visit expenses
- College/Graduate school tuition
- College/Graduate school, room and board (inclusive of decor and food), books, and supplies

- College/Graduate school weekly/monthly allowance (personal expenses)
- Car expenses (driving lessons, legal document fees, purchase/lease/insurance, gas, and repairs)
- Living Will for when the child turns 18
- Guardianship if both parents die
- Designation of Health Care Surrogate form when child turns 18
- Durable Power of Attorney form when child turns 18
- Obligations with respect to a child who might be dependent beyond 18 years of age

The below items do not typically go in a Parenting Plan, but you want to make sure these issues are discussed and agreed upon in writing:

- Child support needs
- Life Insurance to cover child support
- Health insurance
- Unreimbursed medical expenses

Remember: You have the right to ask for custom provisions. If you do not ask, you have no chance of getting what you desire.

Pet ownership Considerations:

- Timesharing arrangements
- Responsibilities
- Financial obligations (vet, pet sitter, food, kennel, grooming, etc.)
- Funeral arrangements

*Growth occurs
outside of your
comfort zone.
Motivate yourself to
seek out new skills
and achievements!*

CHAPTER 14

Financial Piece

A fair and informed *Marital Settlement Agreement* (a contract written and signed by both spouses, that defines the terms of the divorce settlement) depends on you having an accurate picture of your income, expenses, assets, and debts. If you are contemplating divorce, you want to make sure you are keeping track of your account balances. Gathering documents and evidence that can support your claims for alimony, child support, equitable distribution, and other financial issues will make the process more efficient. When it comes to your future, acquiring financial literacy and hiring a qualified professional on your team is critical.

Initial steps:

o Ask your Divorce Coach, therapist, attorney, and friends for **vetted referrals** to Certified Public Accountants (CPA®), Forensic Accountants, Certified Financial Planners (CFP®), Chartered Financial Analyst (CFA®), and/or a Certified Divorce Financial Analyst (CDFA®).

o Consider having a friend or a Divorce Coach accompany you to some or all of the professional meetings. There is a lot to learn and keep track of at the same time as you may be feeling emotional and overwhelmed.

○ Many individuals contemplating divorce prematurely seek out legal assistance prior to understanding their assets, debts, monthly costs, and the children's monthly expenses. Seeking financial advice first can save you time, emotional overwhelm, and money. Spouses often make the decision to get divorced without knowing the financial impact on the marital estate. There are companies that can assist in developing this financial clarity prior to starting legal action and being required to fill out a **financial affidavit.** This document is a sworn statement of your income, expenses, assets, and liabilities that needs to be completed at the beginning of the divorce process to help determine the basis, if any, for alimony and child support. Think of it as the summary of information reflected in the many mandatory disclosure statements you will be asked to gather.

> **My Divorce Solution** (mydivorcesolution.com) is a company that assists individuals and/or couples in developing financial clarity when the dissolution of marriage is on the table. This is often a time when families feel vulnerable and are easily pressured into making uninformed financial decisions based on fear and anxiety. The two founders of My Divorce Solution, a CDFA and a Legal Liaison respectively, both divorced themselves, understand the financial pitfalls experienced during this emotional time and created a valuable tool to guide individuals and/or couples to avoid common mistakes. The mission of the company is to greet the possibility of divorce in a whole new way by helping develop, in a judgment-free space, a transparent and comprehensive financial plan that will optimize the outcome of financial decisions.

The plan is called the **MDS Financial Portrait™**. It is a unique and comprehensive document containing analyzed and summarized financial data, along with key and supporting documents essential in making well-thought-out, comprehensible, and confident financial decisions. The advantage of creating the MDS Financial Portrait™ is that it provides a clear neutral reference point of the marital and non-marital estate for purposes of determining alimony, child support, and the division of assets and liabilities. This affordable and comprehensive Portrait can then be used by divorce professionals, if needed, as verification of marital and non-marital assets. It is also the financial blueprint when considering various scenarios, alternatives, and resulting implications of any financial decisions.

Understand the various financial professionals that can assist you:

○ **Knowledge is power.** Schedule consultations with several professionals to learn about and discuss the best financial process for your case.

1. *Certified Public Accountant (CPA):* A trusted financial advisor who has passed the CPA exam and met work experience requirements in order to be licensed.
2. *Forensic Accountant:* An accountant often brought in for complicated financial cases who uses accounting, auditing, and investigative skills to reconstruct financial history and find hidden assets, liabilities, and income.

3. ***Certified Divorce Financial Analyst: (CDFA®)***: A CDFA® professional is an expert on the financial aspects of divorce. The role of the CDFA® is to help both you and your and attorney understand how financial decisions made today will impact your financial future, based on certain assumptions. This individual provides analysis and support prior, during, and after settlement or trial to help people work toward achieving their goals.

4. ***Chartered Financial Analyst (CFA®):*** An experienced financial analyst who has passed examinations in economics, financial accounting, portfolio management, security analysis, and standards of conduct given by the Institute of Chartered Financial Analysts.

5. ***Certified Financial Planner (CFP®)***: An expert in the financial field who has undergone extensive training and has expertise in areas of financial planning including investment, insurance, retirement, tax, and estate planning.

Obtain Essential Financial Documents:

○ You will want to create a **Master List** of financial documents from at least the past 3 years and where to obtain them. The number of years will depend on what your financial and legal professionals request. When you are able to gather documents and evidence in a comprehensive and logical way, many of the questions and requests for additional information will be minimized. Assembling all of the information will also help you get a much clearer picture of your complete financial situation. Make sure you know:

- Where the **original copy of each document** can be found.
- Where **copies of each document can be located**.
- The **names and contact information of any professional** who help you create the document.
- The **website from which all documents are downloaded** from the internet.
- **Instructions on opening any safe deposit box** into which you may deposit the document.
- How to identify all of your **possessions (videorecord** the contents of your home and anything in a safe).
- Any **personal property** you owned prior to the marriage.

General Categories (documents needed):

Accounts:

- List every **bank account (including money market and CD's) for you, your soon-to-be ex, and the children**, with bank name, account numbers, names on accounts, and whether the bank holds a safe deposit box for you.
- List every **payment account** such as PayPal, Venmo, or Zelle and information on how to gain access (passwords) and/or otherwise deal with those accounts.
- List every **investment, brokerage account, and trust** with the associated institution's name, phone number, and account number (including stock options, stocks, bonds, mutual funds, etc.).
- List every **Personal Retirement Account** including IRA's and Roth IRA.
- List every **employer-sponsored retirement account** including 401(K)/profit-sharing plans, defined contribution plans, 457, 403(B), and SEP.

- Make a list of any military retirement accounts.
- List every **credit card** with the card number, expiration date, the CVV code (card verification value), login, and password information for online account management.
- List every **debit card for you, your soon-to-be ex, and the children** including the ATM card with the card number, authorized users, expiration date, the CVV code (card verification value), and any other information needed to manage any online account associated with it.
- If you do not have a **credit card in your name using your own credit,** consider getting one.
- If you do not have a **checking and savings** account in your individual name alone consider opening one.

Housing/Maintenance Expenses:

- Make a list of **Title/Deed/Lease/Promissory Notes** to your residence(s) and any other real property you own or rent and **property tax documents** (tax bills/receipt for payment).
- Know if there are any **liens** (mortgage, mechanic's, or tax) or any **open building permit**s on the property.
- Make a list of all **maintenance information** for real property you own or rent (for example, let's say you have a chimney; keep records of when you have your chimney swept and who performed the service).
- Make a list of all **mortgages and other loans** with the bank or lender's name, a copy of the loan agreement with the loan number and expiration date, and any information needed to manage any online account associated with the loan. Mortgage closing documents are also helpful since they list assets, liabilities, and sources of income at the time of application. Make sure to also

make copies of the most recent mortgage statement for the marital home and any other properties.

○ Make a copy of **Homeowner's Association** dues or **condo fees**, if any.

○ Make a list of all **household recurring utilities** such as gas, electric, water and sewer, internet, phone (cell and land), cable, garbage, ground maintenance (lawn care, landscaping, tree trimming, & snow removal), fuel oil or natural gas, pressure cleaning, pest control, home security system, generator, reverse osmosis service, annual a/c, duct cleaning, service contracts on appliances, general repairs and maintenance, pest control, swimming pool, etc.

○ Consider getting **property and other assets professionally appraised** before the separation.

Recurring Living Expenses:

○ Make a list of every **recurring living expense** such as school tuition, school supplies, children's activities, cleaning/domestic help, food/groceries, clothing, dry cleaning, tailor, shoe repair, personal care/grooming, pet care, gifts (birthday and holidays), safe deposit box, etc.

Insurance Information:

○ Make a copy of every **insurance policy**, if you have one, and a copy of the most recent account statements outlining the current claims and explanations benefits. Also keep a list of the insurance premium expenses for health insurance, dental insurance, homeowner's/renter's insurance, flood insurance, hurricane insurance, pet insurance, life insurance (cash value accumulation, surrender value, etc.), disability insurance, long-term care insurance, auto insurance, umbrella liability, and other insurance policies (theft, fire, earthquake, etc.).

○ Assess whether you will need to secure new healthcare coverage when the divorce is finalized.

Medical Information:

○ Make a copy of your current **medical and dental insurance plan**. Knowing what the benefits are will allow you to make an educated decision between opting to be on Cobra or obtaining a separate policy.

○ Make a list of all **medical expenses** including insurance premiums from doctors (family doctor, specialist, psychologist, etc.), dentist/orthodontist, drugs, prescriptions, medications, and **other items** such as deductibles and eyeglasses.

Automobile Information:

○ Make a list of all **vehicles you own or lease including the title/deed to your vehicles or** copy of any lease agreement. (loan or lease payments, gas and oil, license/registration, excise taxes, maintenance and repairs, parking fees/tolls, auto club fees, etc.). Kelly Blue Book® new and used car price values are helpful.

Personal Property Information:

○ Make a list of all **credit card points** acquired during the marriage.

○ Make a list of all **reward points** acquired during the marriage (airline, hotel, rental car, etc.).

○ Make a list of all **memorabilia and figurines** acquired during the marriage and appraised values.

○ Make a list of any **season tickets** and values.

- Make a list of **hobby equipment** (guns, tools, etc.)
- Make a list of all **collections** (stamps, letters, coins, cards, etc.) and appraised values.
- Make a list of all **china and decorative plates** acquired during the marriage and appraised values.
- Make a list of all **furniture** acquired during the marriage and appraised values.
- Make a list of all **jewelry** acquired during the marriage and appraised values.
- Make a list of all **artwork** acquired during the marriage and appraised values.
- Make a list of all **antiques** acquired during the marriage and appraised values.
- Make a list of the **wine and liquor collection** acquired during the marriage and appraised values.
- Make a list of all **intellectual property** acquired during the marriage (copyrights, patents, trademarks, research, trade secrets, etc.).
- Make a list of **royalties** earned on books, music, minerals, franchises, etc.
- Make a list of all **digital assets** acquired during the marriage (websites or blogs). Protect your digital footprint.
- Write down information on **storage units.**
- Write down information on pre-purchased **cemetery plots** and figure out a plan.
- Make a copy of **cord blood storage** contract and fees, if any.
- Make a copy of **frozen embryo** storage contract and fees, if any.

Recreational Information:

- Make a list of all **entertainment and recreation expenses** such as lunches, dining out, theatre, movies, concerts, and sporting events, memberships and club dues (health clubs and country clubs), music and other entertainment (iTunes, Netflix, etc.), vacations and weekend trips, hobbies (music lessons etc.), subscriptions (newspapers and magazines), etc.

○ Make a list of **Timeshares** and values.

○ Make a copy of **the title, registration, and value for all owned or leased boats, trailers, motor homes, airplanes, jet skis, etc. Appraisals** are also helpful.

Business Information:

○ Make a copy of the **business valuation**, if you have one.

○ Make a list of **business interests: Entity Creation Documents, Partnership Agreements, Shareholder Agreements, Operating Agreements, and any amendments thereto, etc.**

○ Make a list of **information about you and your soon-to-be ex's employer**: name, address, email, and phone number.

○ List your and your soon-to-be ex's **length of employment and monthly or annual salary.** Make a copy of **recent paystubs.**

○ Make a copy of all **employment contracts.**

○ Make a copy of **employer provided benefits/stock options** (vested and unvested).

○ Make a list of any memberships and dues you or your spouse have to **unions or other professional networking organizations.**

Income Information:

○ Make a list of **earned income**, if any, and the sources such as gross salary and wages, self-employment, etc.

- ○ Make a list of **unearned income**, if any, and the sources such as pensions, social security, interest and dividends, annuities, trusts, partnerships, S Corp distributions, rental property, etc.

- ○ Make a note of **Social Security benefits, disability, unemployment insurance, worker's compensation**, or **other sources of income** such as alimony, child support, inheritance, insurance settlement, etc.

- ○ Make copies of **all investment employer-sponsored retirement accounts and other retirement accounts** (IRA, Roth IRA, etc).

- ○ **Premeditated divorce planning** is something to be aware of. Hiding assets to prevent your soon-to-be ex-spouse from being included in the community property or equitable distribution settlement happens. If there is a concern regarding **financial infidelity** (engaging in any financial behavior that is expected to be disapproved of by one's spouse and intentionally failing to disclose this behavior to the other party), make sure to gather any documentation you can and advise your financial professional. **Hidden assets** include missing bank accounts, offshore accounts, assets in other countries, cash income, assets, trusts, or other entities that are hidden, or assets that are transferred to LLC's, hidden rental income, secret credit cards or stock options, luxury items including jewelry, gold, boats, cars, tools, cash, Cryptocurrency, safe deposit boxes, etc.

- ○ If there is a concern regarding **marital dissipation of assets** (when a spouse is frivolously spending or squandering assets in an attempt to reduce marital property value), make sure to gather any documentation you can and advise your financial professional. Someone could dissipate assets by spending money on a significant other, gambling, etc.

Charitable contributions

○ Make a list of charitable contributions (indicate re-curring or one time).

Inheritance

○ Generally, inheritance is not subject to equitable distribution because it is not considered marital property. Speak with your attorney.

Know How Your Debts Are Titled

○ Whose name is on the debt?
○ Who is, from the lender's perspective, legally obligated to pay it?

Know if there are any outstanding loans and the details:

○ school loans
○ housing loans
○ personal loans
○ business loans
○ any other liability

Tax Information:

○ Make a copy of the most recent **federal and state tax returns.** You should keep copies of your last income tax returns for the current and preceding seven years (in case of audit), along with the supporting docu-mentation (such as W-2, 1099, and k-1).
○ Ask about **federal tax issues** that might need to be addressed such as federal tax return filings, the trans-fer of assets between divorcing spouses, the continu-ing application of favorable tax provisions applicable

to a principal residence, and attorney's fees related to these matters.

o Ask about **income tax expenses** such as federal tax withholding, state tax withholding, city/local tax withholding, social security withholding, federal estimated tax withholding, state estimated tax withholding and Medicare tax withholding).

Additional Action Steps:

o Obtain and make a copy of your recent **credit report**. The document will list your credit history and activity, including any debts.

o Know if there are any **pending lawsuits, judgments, liens, or awards** that can affect the marital estate financially.

o Revaluate, analyze or develop a **comprehensive retirement plan** with the assistance of a financial specialist such as a CDFA®. The plan should be based on your needs, goals, and financial and personal situation. Remember, the goal is to gain clarity, comfort, and financial security.

o Discuss your **long-term care plan**.

o **Arrange for a mailing address that only you can access,** if you are concerned about your soon-to-be ex-spouse or anyone having access to your mail.

o Consider **inflation**, the increase in the prices of goods and services.

o Make sure you understand the **after-tax value of all assets** when dividing up the marital estate.

o **Consider a platform to manage, track, and pay mandated alimony, child support, and additional child expenses** because the management of the financial stipulation often becomes complex, time-consuming, stressful, and expensive. Additionally, it requires constant communication between the parties which often intensifies conflict.

SupportPay (www.supportpay.com) is an example of such a platform and was founded by Sheri Atwood, divorcee, mother, and business executive. It helps individuals to simply and securely make and receive payments, resolve disputes, and generate organized records for taxes or court. It is the first management platform enabling individuals to pay and receive alimony, child support, and additional child expenses such as medical, dental, childcare, educational, and extracurricular expenses directly between each other. SupportPay is an affordable, organized alternative to messy spreadsheets, stacks of receipts, and constant negotiations.

Judges welcome SupportPay users because they are more likely to pay support, avoid future litigation, and present complete and organized support history. The platform can assist parents paying support through state systems who must track and pay other expenses on their own, as well as additional payments due to overtime, bonuses, or commissions. SupportPay can also help high-conflict individuals limit communication with the internal dispute resolution feature integrated within the system. Additionally, victims of domestic abuse can feel comfortable using the system because they avoid disclosing information about their location or bank accounts. Even amicable individuals love SupportPay because reducing conversations about money keeps conflict low.

Using SupportPay will allow you to spend less time managing the fiscal obligations of the martial settlement agreement so you can move forward with your life in a more productive and healthy manner.

Other Business Professionals you might need to consult with if your divorce is more complex:

1. *Actuaries:*
   In the divorce process, you must properly value every marital asset in order to ensure equitable distribution. **Pension and retirement plans** often pose a problem in determining their value. Actuaries and pension experts intimately understand retirement plans and many of the issues divorcing individuals face.

2. *Certified Appraisers:*
   Appraisers can make a difference in your divorce. The marital home and any other real property may be components of the marital estate. In many cases, **the family home is the largest joint asset to deal with** during a divorce. Jewelry, furniture, and art are also often worth appraising. Knowing exactly how much your house and other valuable items are worth is important.

3. *Bankers/Mortgage Brokers/Certified Lending Specialists:*
   These professionals will look at the **mortgage questions that divorce can raise**, offer options, and will provide some advice on handling new home loans, such as refinancing the mortgage. They will help ensure the best outcome possible, seeing the option that makes the most financial sense for you.

4. *Insurance Brokers:*
   A divorcing couple needs to know about their **insurance coverage** during separation, whose insurance will cover the children after the divorce, and how all of the collective insurance policies including life insurance (term and whole), disability insurance, long-term care insurance,

auto insurance, homeowner's or renter's insurance will be affected during or as a result of the divorce.

5. ***Certified Fraud Examiners:***
Fraud is a deceptive action intended for personal or financial gain and a certified fraud examiner is a highly qualified professional who investigates cases of criminal and civil fraud.

6. ***Private Investigators:***
Hiring a private detective agency is one of the ways of reducing the strain and chaos that might come with a divorce. Investigators are hired to help solidify details and facts that may be relevant to your proceedings.

7. ***Vocational Experts:***
A vocational expert will evaluate a spouse in a divorce case to establish his or her employability and earning capacity. The expert will then document the findings from the evaluation in a vocational examination report. The completed document will help the court determine the amount and duration of spousal and child support.

8. ***Real Estate Brokers:***
A couples' inclination to battle over every detail of the home sale is the very reason why they need an agent with **divorce home sale experience**. The right agent becomes the neutral voice of authority on things like pricing, marketing, and what home improvements will actually help the house sell.

You are not defined by what happened to you. Keep evolving!

Section 3

Strategies to Empower You During the Divorce Process

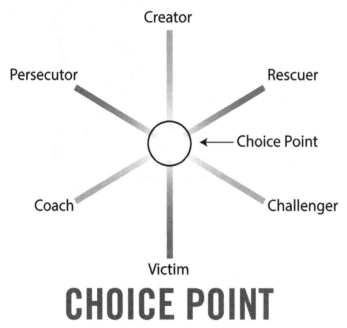

CHOICE POINT

(©David Emerald -- www.powerofted.com – Used with permission.)

Opportunity exists with every challenge. Tap into your strengths. You can do tough things!

CHAPTER 15

Healthy Change and Growth is in Your Control

I f you are contemplating divorce, you are not alone. There are so many challenging decisions that need to be made while emotions are running on overdrive. It is during this period of time that you want to purposefully learn how to hit the pause button to provide you with the opportunity to reflect effectively. Individuals have the tendency to quickly identify a problem and then jump to conclusions in an effort to rectify the situation and to decrease the period of discomfort. Impulsivity during problematic periods can lead to irrational and frantic choices, forced and unfavorable solutions, and increased pain and discomfort.

If you immediately react to an uncomfortable situation, feeling, or event in a state of resistance or misalignment, becoming unstuck is an uphill battle. It is extremely helpful when you have to make difficult decisions to use the framework entitled the **3 A's of Change: Awareness, Acceptance, and Action.** Implementing this three-step process when attempting to solve a problem will become a valuable resource for you. Taking time to move through each stage of the dilemma will enable options to become more visible and will facilitate life-long personal growth and self-development.

AWARENESS:

The initial stage of problem-solving is to create a space for *awareness*. It is essential to take time during this period to give conscious attention to what is going on, how the issue arose, why the situation is triggering you, and how you feel about it. *Awareness* requires aiming to be open to understanding the truth about the problem. It allows you to stand back from the uncomfortable situation with some objectivity. This stage gives you visibility, vison, and a possibility for different choices. It requires asking questions of yourself like:

1. **What is it about this situation that I am not seeing yet?**
2. **What is it about this situation that I am reading into?**
3. **What consequences such as losses or restrictions am I feeling about this situation?**

Intentionally slowing down long enough to get a grasp of the situation, feeling, or event prior to reacting creates opportunity for reflection, openness, and curiosity. It gives you the power to make a thorough investigation of the situation and its impact on you personally before reacting. **There can be no change without *awareness*.**

ACCEPTANCE:

After an appropriate amount of time practicing being *aware*, you are ready to move into the *acceptance* stage. It requires an open and honest examination of the issue despite any discomfort that may arise. *Acceptance* involves honoring and recognizing where you are and who you are in the moment without any resistance. Focusing on accomplishing *acceptance* means that you have an emotional willingness to work through the losses and restrictions stemming from the problem in order to develop clarity. This stage requires additional time for you to take control of your life and to own the choices that are available to you. Some questions you might ask yourself are:

1. **What am I feeling because of this situation?**
2. **What choices can I make that will bring me peace with this situation?**
3. **What do I want to stand for as it relates to this situation?**

Aligning your mind, body, and emotions will provide you an opportunity to move through the challenging situation in a positive way. Once the stages of *awareness* and *acceptance* have been worked through, you can effectively propel yourself forward into action because you will experience an increased feeling of emotional balance and peace of mind.

ACTION:

The *action* stage of the framework is where you create change. It encourages a thoughtful and intentional response to the problem. Rather than a knee-jerk reaction, you allow yourself time to assess your choices and to move forward with a solution that aligns best with your feelings, values, and needs. Questions you might ask yourself during this stage are:

1. **How do I feel about moving through this situation?**
2. **What resources do I need to move through this situation?**
3. **What is the best choice for me in this situation?**

Moving into *action* uses up the energy that was stagnating and naturally makes you feel better. Creating a process to identify your choices and to act accordingly is extremely empowering.

Everyone has the ability to define for themselves the difference between what is acceptable and comfortable and what is not. Implementing the **3 A's of Change: Awareness, Acceptance, and Action** when times become challenging fosters understanding, reflection, question seeking, acknowledgement, and the ability to move into action in a productive and forward manner. The three-step framework brings your mind, body, and emotions together and guides you to experience a well-thought-out response to a given situation. By taking these steps, options become more visible, and you foster a course of action and an attitude that effectuates change and personal growth.

Healthy Change and Growth is in Your Control

*How can you use the **3 A's Framework** to help you change and grow?*

_____

_____

_____

_____

_____

_____

_____

_____

_____

_____

_____

_____

_____

_____

_____

_____

_____

_____

107

Talk to yourself in a supportive and loving way. Be your own inspiration!

CHAPTER 16

The Vocabulary You Use Impacts Your Self-Esteem

How familiar are you with your internal dialogue? The language you use can have a profound impact on your self-image, how you show up in the world, and how you live your life. Words have the power to shape your beliefs and influence your decisions. The way you express yourself, your choice of words, and tone of voice creates energy that either gives you power or takes it away. Speech has the ability to change perception. Making the conscious choice to eliminate disempowering words from your vocabulary can be transformative.

The language you choose can be limiting. You can change your beliefs by being mindful of how you talk. People often use disempowering words such as **can't, have, need, should, never, always, try, and but**. Negative words are taken for granted as part of your everyday communication and narrows your mind in a way that cuts you off from other options and possibilities. Additionally, disempowering words have an effect on your feelings and behaviors. They diminish your ability to be the master of your destiny, create discomfort, and decrease the amount of energy you have to move forward in a fulfilling way.

Why set the intention of consciously choosing to use empowering vocabulary? Implementing positive language will shift your energy levels, elevate your power, and help reduce resentment and drama in your life. It will also enhance your ability to be a creator instead of a victim. You will become more open to options you didn't see before. Utilizing empowering language can enhance the strength and motivation you need to keep moving forward.

You can begin eliminating disempowering words by identifying them and choosing to reframe your language in a more positive manner.

Disempowering: CAN'T	*Empowering: WON'T*

CAN'T: When you say, "I can't," you set yourself up for failure because it means that you are giving up or that you lack the power. It implies a low self-image, helplessness, and a lack of self-control. Using the word also increases your stress level, blocks creativity, and hinders your ability to problem solve.

WON'T: When you say, "I won't," you assert confidence and self-control. It signifies preference and choice.

Disempowering: HAVE /NEED	*Empowering: CHOOSE /WANT*

HAVE TO/NEED TO: When you say, "I have to or I need to," you are relinquishing your ability to make your own choices and therefore become a victim. Using those words fosters the inner dialogue that creates conditions of powerlessness. Everything is a choice. You don't "have to." You "do," or "get to do."

CHOOSE TO/WANT TO: When you say, "I choose to or I want to," you acknowledge that you have the right to select your path.

Disempowering: SHOULD	Empowering: CAN/COULD

SHOULD: When you say, "I should," it implies there is a right or wrong way to do something. Thinking you might be wrong is not elevating. It sends a message that you are not in control or worthwhile and don't want to do something. The word "should" also signifies a lack of acceptance rather than encouragement.

CAN/COULD: When you say, "I can or I could," you are reinforcing your freedom and ability to take full ownership.

Disempowering: ALWAYS/NEVER	Empowering: SOMETIMES/ OFTEN/ SELDOM

ALWAYS/NEVER: When you say, "always or never," you are trying to prove a point and become position-based. Your goal becomes winning instead of understanding and positive resolution. These words encourage awfulizing and catastrophizing thoughts which deplete your energy and cause anxiety.

SOMETIMES/OFTEN/SELDOM: When you say, "sometimes, often, or seldom," you do not box yourself in; rather, you create opportunity for openness and acceptance.

Disempowering: BUT	Empowering: AND

BUT: When you say, "but," it causes everything that was said or thought before it to be negated. It often has the effect of changing a neutral statement into a negative one. The word closes off the conversation space or thought process.

AND: When you say, "and," it enables you and others to stay focused on your intentions and true to what you want to say or do. It allows you to remain more open and less defensive.

Disempowering: TRY	*Empowering: COMMIT*

TRY: When you say, "I try," it means that you are unsure, indecisive, and disengaged from the commitment. It makes it okay to fail without a fight.

COMMIT: When you say, "I commit," you make a pledge that obligates you to a certain course of action. You work harder; you look for solutions when faced with obstacles; you don't consider quitting as an option, and you don't look back. Commitments are empowering because they influence how you think, how you sound, and how you act.

Speaking a positive vernacular requires constant awareness. There are four strategies to help you succeed:

1. **Be present**: When you catch yourself using disempowering words, don't shame yourself. Just remember sooner next time. Consistently congratulate yourself when you use empowering words.
2. **Practice**: Using positive words can become more habitual with practice. Some helpful activities

include reciting positive affirmations in the morning or doing mirror exercises daily to reinforce the use of empowering words.

3. **Shift**: Identify disempowering words you would like to omit from your vocabulary and focus on the empowering words that will help to reframe your perspective, feelings, or understanding of a situation.

4. **Focus on the benefits**: Use self-talk to clarify how using empowering language allows you to feel healthier and more accepting.

Using the four strategies habitually will enable you to replace disempowering words with a more helpful and productive dialogue.

Any word that creates the illusion that you don't have a choice disempowers you. Removing negative words from your vocabulary takes time, patience, and practice. It is possible and comes with great rewards. Consciously implementing empowering words makes any situation more tolerable, broadens and builds possibilities, and opens your mind to be able to speak from a place of choice and control. It helps reframe reality so that any situation can be more tolerable and enjoyable. The option is yours. Challenge yourself to speak with power to bring out the best in yourself and others.

*How will you use your words to **empower yourself**?*

_____

_____

_____

_____

_____

_____

_____

_____

_____

_____

_____

_____

_____

_____

_____

_____

_____

Look for the positive messages in every mess. There are no failures, only lessons!

CHAPTER 17

Minimizing Conflict is a Choice

If you are contemplating or ending your marriage, there will be many changes occurring in your life that can lead to confusing and overwhelming challenges. Conflict between partners at this time is very normal. It is common to have numerous heated arguments while living through a time of hurt, loss, and anger. When emotions are high, the ability to articulate yourself without escalating the situation is difficult. Finding ways to manage and keep conflict at a minimum is essential during this period of time. If you can express your feelings in a way that does not attack, blame, or criticize, you are less likely to provoke defensiveness and hostility in the other person, which tends to intensify disagreements. You also have a better chance of the other individual not shutting down or tuning you out, which can often stifle communication. It is important to remember that everyone desires to be understood and appreciated, especially when emotions are high. True sources of conflict can be diminished or resolved in a healthier manner by practicing **"I" messages** and an **EAR™ Statement** because these skills can help you voice your concerns, feelings, and needs in a manner that shows Empathy, Attention, and Respect to the other person.

For healthy communication, the goal with any disagreement must be to move through the conflict in a civil way while attempting to reach a reasonable resolution. Being conscious of how you react or respond to an individual expressing intense emotions must be strategic in nature. While focusing on the problem at hand and implementing "I" statements, it is essential to be mindful of not putting yourself in a position of defending yourself. The simple technique called an EAR™ Statement can be practiced to calm individuals down and helps you connect with the person's feelings and experience.

E mpathy: The ability to understand, relate, or share the feelings of another. Everyone has experienced pain or frustration at one point in life.

A ttention: Noticing someone or something. Attention can be shown through words, good eye contact, nodding of the head, leaning in, physical closeness, or touch.

R espect: Admiration for someone or something elicited by their abilities, qualities, or achievements. Even difficult people have some quality you can admire.

Utilizing an EAR™ statement is the opposite of what you feel like giving someone when they are verbally upset and attacking you. However, when used correctly, the technique is helpful in setting limits on misbehavior or a difficult conversation such as giving bad news. The EAR™ Statement also allows you to maintain an arm's length relationship which can be extremely reassuring when conflict is arising.

During difficult conversations, individuals often become position-based, emotionally attack those closest to them, and exhibit intense frustration. Implementing 'I" messages and an EAR™ Statement can be used in person, over the phone, or in writing. The skills place an emphasis on being conscious of the words, tone of voice, and body language you use while involved in an argument or heated conversation. Below are examples of wording you can use when implementing an EAR™ statement. Keep in mind, the strategy does not need to communicate all three of the elements each time. Often, showing respect is enough.

E mpathy: (validation)
- "I can see how frustrated you are by the situation."
- "Wow, I can hear how upset you are."
- "I can see how important this is to you."
- "I understand this can be frustrating."

A ttention: (consideration)
- "Let's talk about it so I can really understand what's happening."
- "Tell me what is going on."
- "I will listen carefully."
- "You have my undivided attention."

R espect: (acknowledgement)
- "I have a lot of appreciation for the efforts you have made to deal with this issue."
- "You have important skills that we need here to solve this problem."
- "I can see that you are working hard to come up with solutions."
- "I admire your commitment to solving this issue."

Incorporating the "I" messages and a complete EAR™ Statement over time and with consistent practice will help to diffuse the intensity of conflict between the individuals involved.

Even in the best cases, going through a divorce is difficult. Creating more opportunities for conflict resolution by implementing constructive dialogue is essential. Applying an EAR™ Statement technique and using "I" messages doesn't mean that you believe or agree with the other person. Your goal is to deescalate the conflict by calming the other person down enough to talk about solving the problem or helping the upset individual feel better so that a meaningful conversation can develop. This is not a foolproof strategy, and some individuals remain angry or are just too overwhelmed to settle down; however, it is often successful. Practicing skills that have the opportunity to foster effective dialogue and less intense conflict are critical to moving through the divorce process.*****

***** (Eddy, 2018)

*How can you incorporate **"I" messages and an EAR™ statement** to enhance your conflict resolution skills?*

_____

_____

_____

_____

_____

_____

_____

_____

_____

_____

_____

_____

_____

_____

_____

_____

*You have the power
to manage your
mindset. Be willing
to shift!*

CHAPTER 18

The Importance of a Daily Check-In

A positive way to start each day is to check-in with yourself. Developing this habit will come more easily if you identify a current habit you already do each morning, like brushing your teeth, and then stack your new behavior before or after it. The reason that **habit stacking** is so successful is that your current habits are already locked into your brain from continued patterns and behaviors you have repeated over time. By linking a new habit to one that is already built into your brain, you make it more likely for the new habit to stick. **Remember, what you focus on expands.**

A beneficial new habit to start during the divorce process is to ask yourself the below 2 questions each morning before/after brushing your teeth:

1. What can I do to feel healthy today?
2. What do I want to do to make today a good day?

Likewise, it is empowering to ask yourself the below question each evening before/after brushing your teeth:

1. What is at least one thing I am grateful for today?

Remember, **you are worthy of all good things**, and you have the ability to set the tone for your day. Creating the intention to empower yourself at the beginning and at the end of your day is one of the best ways to feel grounded and more optimistic. [******]

[******]   (Clear, n.d.)

*What habits do you want to develop that can be supported more easily with the **habit stacking** technique?*

_____

_____

_____

_____

_____

_____

_____

_____

_____

_____

_____

_____

_____

_____

_____

_____

_____

_____

_____

Trust your gut feelings and follow the spark inside yourself. Keep moving!

CHAPTER 19

The Value in Living Your T.R.U.T.H.

Are there times when you feel disconnected from your truth? If so, you are not alone. Many people going through divorce or other life challenges look outside of themselves for confirmation of how to interpret their intuition or consciously indulge in behaviors that deviate from their own value system. When these patterns develop, your ability to think logically gets weaker over time and you begin to consistently question how to trust or interpret your emotions. As a result, you can become numb or overtaken with fear or uncertainty and consequently live in a state of self-doubt, which separates you from your own feelings. By quieting your mind and focusing on the **T.R.U.T.H. Framework** of Trust, Reflect, Understand, Talk, and Honor, you can connect to your thoughts and feelings and live a more authentic life.

TRUST:

There is no one more important to trust than yourself. There are many layers of self-evaluation and acceptance that can be strengthened over time with focused intention. Believing that you are capable of handling painful emotions, failure, or rejection is key to developing self-trust. Having conviction of your capability can build up your confidence, make it easier for you to make decisions, reduce your stress levels, and lessen your need for approval from others. With conscious action, trust can become more prevalent.

1. **Be yourself:** You are unique and important.
2. **Set reasonable goals for yourself:** Accomplish little goals that point you in the direction of your big goal.
3. **Be kind to yourself:** Be mindful of your self-critical thoughts as they arise. Acknowledge them and let them go. Prioritize loving yourself unconditionally.
4. **Build on your strengths:** Become aware of the things you are good at and attempt other things without judging yourself too harshly. Growth comes from stepping outside of your comfort zone.
5. **Spend time with yourself:** Look inward. Focus on the moment and do your best to fill your love tank.
6. **Be decisive:** Embrace your own power and judgment. Make choices and stick to them.

No one can be as consistently supportive as you can be to yourself. **Trust your inner wisdom.**

REFLECT:

You must want to hop off the treadmill, step back, and reflect on your life, behaviors, and beliefs in order to find your balance in mind, body, and spirit. Being aware of your thoughts and how to uncover your core values and principles is essential to your happiness. Time flies by, and without consciously pausing to evaluate your circumstance, character, actions, and motives, you can feel depleted, stressed, unhappy, frustrated, and tired. In order to connect with your truth, you can set the intention of following these steps:

1. **Stop**: Take a step back from life and allow yourself to take three deep breaths.
2. **Look**: Identify and get perspective on what you notice and see without judgment.
3. **Listen**: Connect to your feelings: your wisest guide. Silently **ask yourself if your thought process, feelings, or actions are hurtful or helpful to you in this moment.**
4. **Act**: Identify the steps you need to take to be one with your truth. Be open to adjusting, changing, or improving.

Taking time for reflection will serve to keep you in check and focused on self-improvements. It will ensure you are as fulfilled as possible while being loyal to your truth.

UNDERSTAND:

It is essential to look within yourself to define and get clarity on what truly aligns with your deepest values. Developing an understanding of what is meaningful to you and making a conscious effort to identify and live by your values will allow you to speak your truth rather than reacting from old, negative patterns. Becoming sympathetic with yourself requires:

1. **Accepting who you are in this moment**: It is normal to struggle or to be disappointed. What is imperative is to focus on bridging the gap between where you are and where you want to be without judgment or blame.
2. **Acknowledging who you are**: Each of us have impulses that drive us. Take time to understand your strengths and weaknesses as well as your personal standards and ethical code.

3. **Define your truth**: Think, meditate, and journal your thoughts and feelings.
4. **Live loud and proud**: Be honest and full in your truth. Be supportive of what is true for you alone and unhindered by outside influences.

Understanding and learning to accept your story and your life will connect you to your truth and will help you develop a deep sensitivity and knowing for how you want to evolve.

TALK (OPENLY):

Communicating what your identity, feelings, needs, boundaries, and desires are in an authentic way is crucial to living in alignment with your inner wisdom. In order to enhance your capacity to speak your truth:

1. **Be honest and name how you feel in the moment**: Communicate care for others. If you feel uncomfortable, scared, resentful, sad, angry, or guilty, identify the emotion. Inner liberation comes from owning your feelings.
2. **Practice acknowledging what you want**: Speak up and step into your life so you can be in truth with what you want. Your desires are a critical part of who you are.
3. **If you have nothing to say, embrace the silence**: Sometimes the best response is to say nothing.
4. **Focus on being real and not on being right**: When someone asks you how you feel, tell the truth. Small moments of authenticity allow you to receive compassion and empathy. Additionally, be mindful not to set the goal of winning or being correct

because that thought process inhibits you from accessing the deepest places of your heart.

5. **Stop managing other people's feelings**: Dominating conversations and people is not productive and doesn't help build authentic communication.

Giving yourself permission to be vulnerable and transparent will enhance and deepen your capacity to speak your truth and will lead to increased freedom, self-respect, and confidence.

HONOR:

Honoring your inner wisdom is the most powerful tool you have for living an authentic life. When you are honest with yourself about what your needs and wants are, and you live a life that is aligned with them, you have a stronger ability to let go of desiring validation by others. Honoring your truth can be really difficult and scary. In order to nurture your inner wisdom, aim to become one with your intuition and allow it to guide you in an appropriate direction:

1. **Be committed to honoring your reality**: Be honest with yourself about yourself.
2. **Become aware of the things you have been avoiding**: Be mindful of the excuses you implement that keep you stuck. Identify and write them down.
3. **Partner with your emotions**: Relax into your feelings of fear or discomfort instead of resisting them. By partnering with your feelings, you decrease the power of the frightening or uncomfortable feelings and allow yourself the ability to honestly explore the depth of your emotions.

4. **Give yourself permission to speak from a place of sincerity**: Hiding or burying your feelings doesn't get you closer to your truth and does not fuel happiness. Be real with your emotions.

5. **Be candid with how you feel**: Do not pretend to feel something you don't. Speak up for yourself and create healthy boundaries. People will treat you the way you allow them to.

6. **Take time to reflect on what truly matters to you**: Pausing allows you time to react in a more positive manner and to keep peace within yourself.

Your truth is your power! Create space to become more aware of your highest principles, values, and desires. Integrity serves everyone in the long run, even if it does not seem that way at first. Being sincere about how you feel what you want or need will allow you to respect yourself as well as others. Consciously plan to validate your inner wisdom, despite any discomfort that might arise. When you stand in your truth, you are honoring your very essence and purpose. True freedom derives from speaking authentically. Go ahead! Take the challenge of embracing a life of liberation and use the **T.R.U.T.H. Framework** to feel empowered and confident.

*How will you aim to live your **T.R.U.T.H.**?*

T.	Trust
R.	Reflect
U.	Understand
T.	Talk
H.	Honor

_____

_____

_____

_____

_____

_____

_____

_____

_____

_____

_____

_____

_____

_____

_____

_____

_____

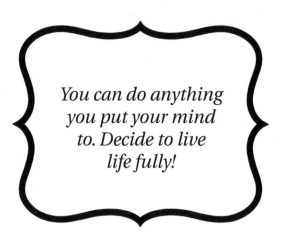

You can do anything you put your mind to. Decide to live life fully!

CHAPTER 20

Remaining C.A.L.M. in Challenging Times is the Way Through

Living life on auto pilot keeps you in your comfort zone and imprisons you at the same time. You keep moving forward, hoping that things will change even when history has proven otherwise. As time slips by, your ability to remain content, calm, and involved decreases while your feelings of resentment, anger, and apathy increase. Setting the intention of developing a conscious and consistent practice of focusing on your breath, slowing down, leaning into awareness, and maintaining positivity is the way through. By focusing on the four steps of the **C.A.L.M. Framework**, you give yourself the time and permission to consciously settle down, develop clarity, react, and problem-solve in a healthy, productive, and more tranquil manner.

CONNECT TO YOUR BREATH

The majority of us rarely think about our breathing. Our face-paced lives cause us to forget that **our breath is a healing tool that is available to us at a moment's notice.** It is important to understand that when you are stressed, your brain doesn't prioritize breathing because it's an unconscious act. You develop an unhealthy upper chest pattern of breathing which is shallow, making it difficult for oxygen to enter. Becoming aware of this unhealthy breathing pattern and intently concentrating on your abdomen breathing helps to connect you to the present moment. This is useful in times of stress, tension, and pain because **when you are focused on the here and now, you are not fixating on the past or future.** Being mindful of the present moment offers your mind a break. It gives you a chance to increase your awareness, choose your thoughts, and become grounded. By understanding the value your breath has in affecting your mood, you can alter your breathing patterns instantaneously by taking deep purposeful breaths for five minutes.

1. **Inhale through your nose for five seconds filling your belly and chest with air.** It is helpful to think of smelling the scent of your favorite flower when inhaling.
2. **Exhale out of your mouth, letting your breath fall out** as if you are blowing out candles on your birthday cake.
3. **Relax for five seconds and repeat.**

By slowing and deepening your breathing, you will manifest feelings of relaxation and calm.

ALLOW TIME TO SLOW DOWN

Situations occur in life that cause extreme reactions. Learning how to save yourself from emotional spirals and thought loops is essential. It is common to fight the negative emotion, flee from it, or attempt to problem-solve your way out of it instead of taking the time to feel and understand its roots. This type of behavior usually ends up expanding the hardship. Emotions can have a strong bodily component that acts as an alarm letting you know something has upset you. Maybe it's nausea, a twisting in the gut, a tightness in the chest, a sensation of warmth running throughout your body, dizziness, or a rapid heart rate. The symptoms are different from person to person and from moment to moment. If you can pause for even the slightest second before anxiety, frustration, or disappointment arises and sweeps you away, your ability to be more mindful about your response or reactions increases significantly. When you consciously interrupt the process by slowing down, you provide yourself the opportunity to collect yourself and to observe what is happening in your mind and body without pursuing it or rejecting it. You have space to just note it without creating a story or any judgment. This behavior tends to de-escalate anxiety. In this space you have several options:

1. **Be with your thoughts and feelings as they are without reacting for at least 10 seconds.**
2. **Keep an open mind and contemplate with calmness.**
3. **Check in with yourself by asking questions such as:**
   - Are these thoughts 100% true? Fact check.
   - Am I exaggerating, projecting, or jumping to conclusions?
   - Am I being closed-minded?
4. **Follow the 3-3-3 rule.**
   Look around you and name three things you see, three sounds you hear, and three things you can touch. This temporary distraction keeps your

thoughts from spiraling and brings you back to the present moment.

5. **Stand straight up.**

   When you are anxious and feel like you are losing control, you have a tendency to hunch your back. If you set the intention of pulling your shoulders back, opening your chest, and standing or sitting with your feet apart, you help your body start to feel that it's back in control.

6. **Do something:**

   Any action that interrupts your train of thought helps you regain a sense of control and presence.

When you slow down and center your mind, you bring yourself back to the present moment. It is in this space where you can react or respond in the most productive and composed manner.

LEAN INTO AWARENESS

Self-awareness is a skill that anyone can learn with practice. It is necessary in taking control of your life, creating what you desire, and manifesting your future. The skill involves paying attention to your inner state and monitoring your stress, thoughts, emotions, beliefs, and body language. In moments of challenge or controversy, being aware of and knowing yourself can make the difference between agitation or tranquility and escalation or resolution. Awareness is the key to the change you desire. It is critical to understand that you always have a choice in what you think. **You are not your thoughts.** You have the autonomy to ruminate catastrophic thoughts while panic and stress increase, or you can think empowering and positive thoughts. In order to become more tranquil, you can consciously release the tension in your muscles, believe that truth is relative, and focus on constructing problem-solving initiatives. Improving your moment-by-moment awareness can be done in several ways.

1. **Self-question: By checking in with yourself and performing daily self-reflection you can cultivate more awareness.**
   o What am I attempting to achieve?
   o What am I doing that is working?
   o What am I doing that is slowing me down?
   o What can I do to change?

2. **Exercise:** Walking or running, especially in the quiet of nature, will provide the opportune time for quiet self-reflection.

3. **Practice mindfulness:** Encourage yourself to be conscious and calm throughout the day, at home, at work, in school, in traffic, in relationships, and in every aspect of your daily life. This is where you create your building blocks of awareness.

4. **Journal:** When you write your thoughts or stream-of-consciousness ideas, you begin opening up to those vulnerable places within and create an opportunity for less reactive communication.

Life can get out-of-control rapidly if you are unaware of how and under what circumstances your emotional nature is triggered. Developing a deeper sense of self-awareness helps you to progress on your personal development journey.

MAINTAIN POSITIVITY

Individuals are continuously faced with difficult situations and temporary setbacks. Uncertainties are unavoidable and inevitable. Studies have shown that having a positive attitude makes your perspective of life seem broad and full of possibilities. If you intentionally choose a positive thought to dwell upon, you keep your mind optimistic and your emotions positive. Your thoughts and feelings will propel you to act in more constructive ways and to keep you moving towards accomplishing your goals. There are many ways to foster positivity in your life:

1. **Start your day with a positive affirmation.**

   In order to build a habit, you must practice it for 21 days. A helpful way to achieve this goal is to wake up each morning and recite or read an affirmation. Intentionally starting the morning with an inspiring mantra sets the tone for the day.

2. **Speak to yourself in a positive manner.**

   The way you talk to yourself is imprinted deeply into your subconscious mind and is more likely to become a permanent part of your self-talk. **"Whatever is expressed is impressed."**

3. **Look for the blessings.**

   Everyone faces adversity and difficulties in life. In order to learn and grow, consciously choose to find something good from every situation. Focus on having **"an attitude of gratitude."**

4. **Move forward towards your goals and dreams.**

Keep your thoughts on your goals, dreams, and on the person you are working towards becoming. **Focus on what wants your heart's attention** and stay in authentic conversation with yourself.

5. **Accept and focus on solutions.**

   Be where you are. Focus on the blessings in your life and the many ways you can move through the challenging situation.

When you resolve to view disappointments as temporary setbacks and as opportunities to learn, you will confront life in a more optimistic way. Having a positive mindset can help you avoid stress. Even out of the most challenging and devastating situations, you can find a silver lining.

Everyone has authority over their own being. Choosing to remain in discomfort, fear, and anger only diminishes life experience. **You can rise despite your challenges just as a bird can learn to fly with a broken wing.** It boils down to making a commitment to yourself to stay awake and open to the present moment. It requires mindfully allowing yourself time to land before responding or reacting to an upsetting event. The stillness will provide the time and reflection needed to bridge the gap between where you are and where you want to be. The **C.A.L.M. Framework** is a tool that you can use wherever you go. By learning how to manage stress and respond with a positive attitude to each challenge, you'll grow as a person, feel more grounded, and step into your future with more direction.

*How will you use the **C.A.L.M. Framework** to settle your soul?*

C. Connect To Your Breath

A. Allow Time To Slow Down

L. Lean Into Awareness

M. Maintain Positivity

Whatever you go through, you grow through. Denying fear does not fix it. Be willing to take risks!

CHAPTER 21

Be *B.R.A.V.E.* and Practice 5 Essential Skills to Alleviate Stress

D ivorce is hard! Stressful times can make you feel out of control, hurt, sad, anxious, fearful, insecure, and powerless. Uncertainty is a part of the human existence. Even though intellectually you know that this time will pass, it is very unsettling. It is important to acknowledge that **you are most malleable when you find yourself in a difficult situation.** Tough times are opportunities for your own personal development. It is essential to question the way you perceive situations that you don't like. If you don't push through your comfort zone, you are likely to repeat the scenario again. Letting go of your former thoughts and behaviors and purposefully following the **5 B.R.A.V.E. Skills** of **B**alance, **R**esilience, **A**utonomy, **V**alor, and **E**mpathy will create the opportunity for change and healing.

BALANCE:

A balanced life is essential for personal effectiveness, peace of mind, and living well. It means creating time for the things you need to do as well as the things you want to do. It is up to you to create harmony between your personal responsibilities while finding time to participate in activities that bring you pleasure, personal fulfillment, and rejuvenation. Make it a priority to nurture yourself while focusing on creating an efficient and positive mindset.

Part of living a well-balanced life is acknowledging how to deal with adversity, unforeseen events, and uncertainty. You have the power to decide how, when, and where to concentrate your energies. Make a list if it will help create structure for you. This rollercoaster will come to an end. Focusing on physical, emotional, and spiritual balance during this unresolved time will reduce your stress, improve your mental state of mind, help boost your energy, and improve your mood. You are in control of what you engage in and how you react. Remember, **your breath is always patiently waiting for you,** so set the intention of focusing on that prior to taking action.

RESILIENCE:

Everyone has varying levels of resilience, but it is a skill you can improve with practice. It requires that you pay attention to your experiences, listen to your emotions, and be open-minded. You can learn from disappointment and failure as well as success and motivation. Your ability to adapt and bounce back during this time will be tested. It is essential, now more than ever, to spend your time and energy identifying and focusing on the things you can control. Putting your efforts where they have the most positive impact will allow you to feel more empowered and confident. **Only you have the ability to decide how you are going to interpret the adversities in your life.** Seek support from your friends and family, embrace the challenge, and stay mindful of your responses. Remember that much of what you are facing is temporary. You have overcome setbacks before, and you can do it again!

AUTONOMY:

Nothing gets you to depend on yourself more than fear or stress. The divorce process is complicated. It is of the utmost importance to deliberately act on your own values and interests. Think about what really matters to you and how you can move through this in the healthiest way possible. Take charge and become a creator of how the days will unfold instead of a victim of the situation. The choice belongs to you. You are capable of making rational and informed decisions on your behalf. In this moment, it is essential to be self-aware, self-reflective, and to self-manage in order to fully maximize your potential. Establish and write down your personal visions and goals. You can use them as affirmations or friendly reminders of your intentions. **You are moving through your suffering when you develop a stronger belief in yourself and your capabilities.**

VALOR:

Hardships can be debilitating and painful. Going through a divorce requires courage and strength. Deliberately strive to find a level of acceptance for the circumstance. The only way to diminish fear and stress is to move through them, face what you have a tendency to avoid, and keep persevering despite your desire to freeze. If you allow yourself to stay stuck in your misery or anxiety, you cannot grow, and the situation has no opportunity to be different. Learn to say NO, ask for what you want, let go of little negativities that weigh you down, and practice defying the status quo. **Just because things have always been a certain way doesn't mean that they will remain the same.** Aim to confront the challenges and fears you are facing and allow your valor to drive your responses and decisions. With forward movement will come empowerment and resolution.

EMPATHY:

No one wants to be in a constant war zone! Divorcing couples must take the time to practice empathy. Not only does it result in a greater level of harmony, but it can also resolve conflict and disagreements more quickly. It is important to understand that true empathy works in two ways. First, it is about nurturing the ability and desire to have compassion for someone else. It requires being open-minded to the feelings and experiences of another. Empathy also involves working on setting aside your own personal biases, opinions, agendas, beliefs, as well as making a conscious choice to accept the other person as they are for who they are - flaws and all. Second, empathy is practicing having the self-awareness needed to better understand yourself, your motives, your emotions, and the effect you have on the other person through your words, actions, and behavior. Only you can decide how to get through this period with the most peace. **Everyone wants to be heard and acknowledged.** Set the objective of being mindful of your body language, tone of voice, eye contact, and the words you choose. You have the power to make conscious choices which will guide you through this taxing period.

Encourage yourself to remain open to new thoughts and behaviors and nurture your ability to forge ahead in a healthier direction. Allow yourself the permission to feel the feelings that come up during this difficult time and the opportunity to move through them in a productive way. Looking from a different angle and consciously deciding what you want to do is the first step in taking your power back. **You have control over how you react when you encourage yourself to look at a challenging situation with objectivity and strategically decide what you want for yourself.** Using the **5 B.R.A.V.E. Skills** will give you the framework you want to follow so that you can move on stronger and more confident.

*How can you implement the **5 B.R.A.V.E. Skills Framework** to push through your own self-limiting boundaries?*

B. Balance

R. Resilience

A. Autonomy

V. Valor

E. Empathy

_____

_____

_____

_____

_____

_____

_____

_____

_____

_____

_____

_____

_____

_____

_____

_____

_____

_____

Everything has potential. Take charge and follow the wisdom of your heart!

CHAPTER 22

L.E.A.N. into Uncertainty for a More Fulfilling Life

Most people like stability, routine, and a sense of control over their lives. Individuals crave some steady ground to walk on, assurance that everything will be alright, a desire for safety and security, and the knowledge of how life will play out. One thing is for sure: experiencing uncomfortable emotions and uncertainty is a natural part of life. During challenging periods such as divorce, it is important to take the time to sit with the uncertainty and to focus on what can be controlled. Acting impulsively to escape or deny the discomfort has the potential of causing additional detrimental consequences. Intentionally shifting to more adaptive and healthier strategies to deal with uncertainty can teach important life lessons that lead to a more peaceful and productive life. The **L.E.A.N. Framework (Let it Be, Empower, Accept, and Nourish)**, when implemented, creates an awareness of the skills necessary to move through the adversity in an effective way.

LET IT BE:

It is okay to allow yourself the time to hurt or be sad. Letting go of difficult situations is often too much to ask, but striving to **let things be as they are** in order to move past them is much more manageable. Holding on to negativity impedes your personal growth and the ability to move forward. Wishing things were different also will not make them so. In order to move through a challenging situation and just let it be, it is essential to focus on the following actions:

Stop blaming others.
It is up to you to take responsibility for your own happiness. Start living the life you imagine and desire.

Make a conscious choice to free yourself.
Mindfully plan to write a decision statement and detail the benefits you will receive from it. Print, post, and read the statement frequently. Your subconscious mind and the intentional behavior will begin to manifest itself naturally and guide you internally to move through the strenuous situation.

Trust you will be okay.
Think of instances in the past where you have felt a similar way and remember how you moved through it. Also, lean on friends and reach out to others you respect because chances are, they have gone through similar experiences.

Create moments of quiet.
Take the time to pause and to focus on what can be learned from the experience. Stillness allows you to hear your inner voice and to create positive action.

You have a choice not to ruminate on things that are out of your control. When you experience that you can let things be that you thought you needed to hold onto, you allow life to teach you instead of remaining stuck.

EMPOWER:

You have the capability of making decisions and handling the various situations that might come your way. It is essential to see yourself as a valuable human being. Feeling like you have little power to change things is a mindset that can undermine your physical and emotional mental health. That type of **"Stinking Thinking"** is extremely disempowering and keeps you stuck. Managing your expectations, taking risks to move you forward, and facing reality will help you see how your challenges are rarely as bad as you thought they would be. When you find yourself in situations over which you feel you have little or no control, encourage yourself to attempt the following actions:

Look for the good that does exist.
There is usually a way to shift your mindset to see something positive in a situation.

Before reacting to others, practice pausing so you do not take their behaviors personally.
Giving yourself a quiet moment enhances your ability to problem-solve.

Focus on staying in your own power by remaining calm even when others aren't.
This is the time to consciously take deep breaths, monitor your body language, and choose your words wisely.

Ask for what you believe you desire and set healthy boundaries.
Remember, people treat you the way you allow them to.

Be mindful of not making requests of people who are incapable of responding appropriately.
Know who you can trust.

Make yourself a priority.
Do things for yourself that bring you joy. Plan time for just you by establishing your goals and needs.

Recognizing your importance and ability to be a creator instead of a victim requires maintaining control over your thoughts. **You have incredible power within yourself!**

ACCEPT:

It can be extremely difficult to accept the present moment without an intense desire to change it. However, when you make a conscious effort to stop fighting reality and to stop resenting that certain aspects of your life aren't the way you want them to be, you leave a space for acceptance to arise. Your control lies in pausing to explore what you are feeling as well as recognizing what is and where you can act and respond accordingly. Setting the objective to achieve acceptance can be manifested in the following ways:

Prior to reacting to a challenging situation, notice when you are fighting or resisting reality.
When you are feeling bitter, resentful, unhappy, or disillusioned, it is an opportune time to explore those feelings in a curious, non-judgmental way.

Make an internal commitment to stop fighting what is.
Denying reality makes it difficult to focus on how to change the situation and creates suffering. By ranting, raving, judging, and blaming, you waste physical and

emotional energy and get nowhere. **Acceptance is not approval. It is simply acknowledging the reality of a situation.** As best as you can, turn your mind toward focusing on how to cope with the challenge. Decide that you have choices to move beyond the present moment and ease your pain so you can consider how to handle the reality before you.

Use your body to help guide you.
Focus on your breath and on relaxing the muscles in your shoulders, face, and stomach. When you are stressed, your body becomes tense. Aiming to relax will allow you to think more clearly.

Encourage yourself to act as if you are accepting (acknowledging, not approving) the situation.
Fighting reality only intensifies your emotional reaction and creates suffering. **You may experience pain, but suffering is optional.** The process of acknowledging what is lets emotions arise and helps you move through a difficult period so you can develop a plan of action and move on.

Focus on coming to terms with the reality of the situation.
The critical thing is to understand that acceptance takes practice, and it might feel uncomfortable and difficult at times. Setting the goal of acknowledging reality, not denying it or fighting it, can create the opportunity for problem-solving and healing.

NOURISH:

Taking care of yourself is essential, especially when going through a period of uncertainty. Often individuals let life happen to them without stopping to check in with themselves on a daily basis. Making self-care a priority allows you to connect to your own sense of meaning and enhances strength and resiliency during challenges times. Acting supportive and encouraging towards yourself requires focusing on the following skills:

Find comfort in daily rituals like meditation. It can enhance your ability to feel steady, centered, or at peace.
Meditation helps you to relax and gain clarity; it provides you with the inner strength to move through a challenging situation. It can also help you stay calm and positive when things get out of control because it gives your mind a rest and allows your thoughts and emotions to settle down naturally so you can process more purposefully.

Make self-compassion a priority because it will allow you to feel more grounded and comforted during difficult times.
Practicing mindful self-compassion gives you time to be in the present moment with your thoughts and feelings. Not only will it provide you with the opportunity to sit with your pain and understand its source, but it will also help you to create a space for you to face the truth of your experience.

Set the goal of focusing on what is good.
You are more likely to fixate on what might go wrong then what might go right. Being afraid is natural, but it only adds fuel to negative thoughts. Encourage yourself to look for the silver linings and the ways you can be grateful. **Set the intention of consciously having a**

mindset of sufficiency instead of scarcity. When you take time to appreciate those constructive things, you help your brain slow down negative thoughts. During this time, the brain releases serotonin, which gives you a mood boost, and dopamine, which encourages your brain to keep looking for things to appreciate.

Feed your body with wholesome foods like fruits, vegetables, nuts, seeds, whole grains, and healthy fats. Nutrition plays a critical role in your mental health. Eating a nutritious diet helps you keep a healthy body weight and a healthy heart. It also reduces your risk of developing some chronic diseases. By aiming to supply your body with a healthy diet, you are giving your brain the fuel it needs to affect your cognitive processes and emotions in a positive way.

Move as much as you can.
Daily physical activity is healthy for your body and mind. People who exercise regularly tend to do so because it gives them a sense of well-being and accomplishment. They feel more energetic throughout the day, sleep better at night, have sharper memory, and feel more relaxed and positive about themselves and their lives. Exercise also relieves stress, improves memory, and boosts your overall mood and health.

Practice kindness or reach out to a close friend or family member when you are feeling stressed or worried.
Getting out of your head and having positive interactions with others releases oxytocin and helps to elevate your mood.

There are frequently opportunities to learn new skills, accept your feelings, tolerate distress, and to move forward despite not knowing what the future holds. In truth, you live with not knowing every single day. It is important to allow yourself the space to feel your emotions, acknowledge the reality of them, and to take action to discover how to handle them. **The answers will come as you walk through the process.** Your journey will unfold, and you will be able to handle the realities that come your way. Setting the objective of using the **L.E.A.N. Framework** will enhance your ability to move through periods of uncertainty in a more effective and beneficial way.

*How will you **L.E.A.N.** into uncertainty in a productive way?*

L. Let It Be

E. Empower

A. Accept

N. Nourish

_____

_____

_____

_____

_____

_____

_____

_____

_____

_____

_____

_____

_____

_____

_____

_____

_____

_____

*Be the author of
your personal story.
Carefully select
thoughts and actions
that drive you
towards your goals!*

Section 4

Mindful Checklists to Foster Well-Being and to Move You Forward During Divorce

MINDSET MATTERS

(Marks, The Wellness Society. Used with permission.)

Champion self-compassion. There is only one you!

CHAPTER 23

Ways You Can Boost Your Self-Confidence During the Divorce Process

- Care for yourself
- Visualize yourself as you want to be
- Set aside some quiet time daily to focus on your goals
- Write and hang up some of your positive traits and accomplishments
- Question your inner critic
- Set a small goal and achieve it
- Groom yourself
- Invest in an item that makes you feel attractive
- Accept compliments
- Think positive
- Sign up for something with a finish line
- Focus on your blessings
- Shift negative thoughts
- Be kind and generous to yourself
- Know your principles and live by them
- Stand tall
- Change a small habit
- Read inspirational books
- Listen to a self-help podcast
- Focus on solutions
- Smile
- Practice positive self-talk
- Spend time in nature

- Change the passwords on your electronic devices to encouraging words
- Exercise
- Empower yourself with knowledge
- Do something you have been procrastinating
- Volunteer
- Go out and be social
- Surround yourself with positive people
- Keep a journal of your achievements
- Create a challenge for yourself and then meet it
- Become a mentor
- Spend time with a pet
- Surround yourself with quotes and pictures that lift you up
- Say NO!
- Immerse yourself in fun activities
- Focus on something you know you do well
- Attempt something you have never done before
- Create personal boundaries

*What other ideas do you have to boost your **self-confidence**?*

_____

_____

_____

_____

_____

_____

_____

_____

_____

_____

_____

_____

_____

_____

_____

_____

_____

_____

_____

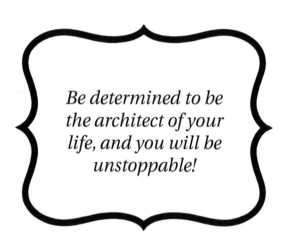

Be determined to be the architect of your life, and you will be unstoppable!

CHAPTER 24

Affirmations to Empower You through the Divorce Process

Allowing what you want to be your truth even if it isn't in this moment leads to empowerment. You can transform your self-image by setting the intention of embracing the influence positive thinking can have on your life experience.

"I AM" Affirmations

Positive "I am" mantras help you speak power into your life and will help you feel more in control. Negative "I am" statements just keep you stuck and away from your destiny. It is very difficult to bring out the positive when you are acting against yourself. **A valuable skill to learn is that whatever follows "I am" will help to determine what your experience will be**. Below are some examples:

○ I am enough.
○ I am grounded.
○ I am strong.
○ I am open to the beauty and gifts of the universe.
○ I am abundant.
○ I am grateful for everything.
○ I am powerful.
○ I am exactly where I am meant to be.

- I am getting closer to my true self each day. Every obstacle, loss, and success brings me closer to that goal.
- I am learning valuable lessons from myself every day, and I will continue to keep learning from myself.
- I am going to take three breathing breaks to calm my soul today.
- I am the architect of my life. I build its foundation and choose its contents.
- I am still the same genuine and attractive person I was when I got married.
- I am courageous, and I can stand up for myself.
- I am fully capable of being alone right now, and I'm okay.
- I am lovable and able to love.
- I am a work in progress and am constantly improving.
- I am capable of making healthy decisions for my personal and spiritual evolvement.
- I am blessed with an incredible family and wonderful friends.
- I am a good person with a lot to offer.

General Affirmations

- I trust myself to make the right decision.
- I allow myself to release all that no longer serves me.
- I give myself space to grow and learn because I understand that there is always room for growth in my life.
- I choose to be happy and hopeful even though it may seem too difficult.
- I love myself exactly as I am right now.
- It's ok to feel lost at times. This is only a temporary situation.

- Change is the only constant, and I will move through this with grace and ease.
- Today, I will focus on joy. I can use this emotion to motivate myself throughout the day.
- My body is healthy, and I am mentally strong.
- My life is full of grace, beauty, and pleasure.
- I will calmly observe my emotions with complete mindfulness.
- My body is open to love and goodness.
- I have the ability to consciously shift my negative thoughts.
- I have been given endless talents, and I have the confidence to use them in a productive way.
- I allow myself to be who I am without judgment because that is what is going to help me to be happiest in my life.
- I listen to my intuition and trust my inner guide because that is going to get me closer to what makes me truly happy.
- I allow pleasure, play, and sensuality into my life.
- My obstacles are moving out of my way.
- My drive and ambition help me to achieve my goals.
- My ability to conquer my challenges is limitless.
- My potential to succeed is infinite.
- I have strength in my heart and clarity in my mind that give me the ability to make good decisions.
- I permit myself to do what is right for me because that is how I allow myself to be the most authentic.
- I acknowledge my self-worth and am willing to improve in areas that I consider weaknesses right now.
- I make a difference in the world by simply existing in it and attempting to make it a better place.
- I welcome the new.
- Divorce is not the end of the road.

- I have an opportunity now to create the life I want.
- Creating a new life is an exciting opportunity.
- I have a bright future ahead of me.

*What other **affirmations** could you use to **empower** yourself?*

_____

_____

_____

_____

_____

_____

_____

_____

_____

_____

_____

_____

_____

_____

_____

_____

_____

_____

_____

It is not selfish to love yourself. It is crucial!

CHAPTER 25

Ways to Practice Self-Care During and After Divorce

○ See a Divorce Coach
○ Close your eyes and breathe deeply for one minute
○ Stretch or foam roll for five minutes
○ Dance
○ Take a long walk in nature
○ Go for a run
○ Follow a daily schedule
○ Keep a gratitude journal
○ Talk with your family
○ Go out with friends
○ Take downtime
○ Unplug
○ Start one small, healthy new habit
○ Be patient and compassionate with yourself
○ Set aside time to explore new interests
○ Get your hands in the dirt. Work in a garden
○ Use a stress-relieving essential oil blend
○ Pick or buy a bouquet of fresh flowers for your home
○ Order in dinner
○ Watch the clouds float by
○ Look at the stars
○ Give yourself permission to take a mental health day
○ Go for a drive — no destination required
○ Sing at the top of your lungs to your favorite music
○ Wear an outfit that makes you feel great

- Watch the sun rise or set
- Go to bed early or sleep late
- Join a support group
- Journal your feelings
- Practice mindfulness
- Eat healthy food
- Solve a puzzle
- Use an adult coloring book
- Soak in a warm bath and light candles
- Give things you no longer use or need to a shelter
- Practice some spiritual activity
- Get a good night's sleep
- Get fresh air
- Have a glass of wine
- Watch a romantic comedy
- Work on a personal project
- Take yourself out for a meal
- Follow new inspirational accounts on social media
- Watch a documentary
- Listen to music
- Take a nap
- Read a new book
- Sit in the sun
- Dress up
- Prepare a meal with a new recipe
- Binge watch your favorite TV show
- Create a vison board
- Make yourself a priority
- Do what feels good to you

*What other ways could you **practice self-care**?*

_____

_____

_____

_____

_____

_____

_____

_____

_____

_____

_____

_____

_____

_____

_____

_____

_____

_____

Be fearlessly authentic. Your future is depending on you!

CHAPTER 26

Tips to Enhance Your Internal Validation: Be Part of Your Support System

1. Avoid judging yourself.
- Be aware of when you get triggered about something that makes you feel less than or insecure.
- Give yourself permission to feel your emotions without judgement. Let your emotions and feelings be what they are.
- Get in the habit of telling yourself, "I have a right to feel how I feel."
- Set the objective of not letting your frustration feed shame.
- Avoid reacting to the feelings that come up. Consciously choose to validate them and sit with the feelings.
- Turn to praise instead of shame. It is extremely validating to praise yourself for what you did do right and the fact that you tried. Tell yourself you are actually doing just fine.
- Practice embracing life. Things often turn out in ways we don't expect and didn't ask for. Practice rationalizing with yourself by saying, "Okay, my feelings are valid, and I am going to have to take this for what it is."

2. Identify what you want.

○ Learn to be in touch with what you yearn for. Speak to yourself as lovingly as you would a small child or your best friend.

○ Become aware of identifying your unmet emotional wounds and how you can start meeting them yourself in the present moment. Understand that your unmet emotional desires can all be met by you, given time and practice. Repeat this process as often as you can and make the act of meeting your emotional desires a top priority in your life.

○ Offer acknowledgement to yourself instead of seeking external validation. Ask yourself, "What do I hope that person tells me?" Then tell yourself.

○ Get in the habit of asking yourself, "What do I want physically right now?"

○ Practice self-compassion.

○ See yourself as the parent to the child version of you.

○ Make a section in your gratitude journal entitled, "You." Write down your accomplishments and celebrate your victories. When you get in the habit of praising yourself, self-validation becomes a habit.

○ Avoid negative self-talk.

3. Focus on your strengths.

○ Come up with self-validating statements such as, "Change can be difficult. I am capable of making the changes necessary to improve my life."

○ Build awareness about the negative voice inside your head and how you criticize yourself. Start a habit of writing the thoughts down. Next, come up with another sentence to replace the initial one, keeping in mind the following question: "What would someone who loves themselves do, think, or write?" Keeping this sentence in mind replaces your initial critical thoughts with more loving, considerate, and empathetic statements.

○ Practice using kind words with yourself.
○ Catch yourself when you are ruminating or overthinking and reframe those thoughts into more rational and mindful ones to help move you forward.
○ Read motivating things.
○ Surround yourself with inspirational people. When you spend time with positive people, you're more likely to be inspired yourself.

Your relationship with yourself is the most important connection that you will ever have. In what other ways can you practice investing time and energy into internally **validating yourself?**

_____

_____

_____

_____

_____

_____

_____

_____

_____

_____

_____

_____

_____

_____

_____

_____

_____

You can rise above any situation or struggle. Trust that you can soar!

A Note from the Author

You are the most valuable person to yourself. Your journey through life is yours to create. **Set the intention of following your inner whispers as they are your GPS.** There is no better moment than the one you are in right now. The fear will not go away until you confront it. Start where you are with a growth mindset. The path is created by taking **one brave bite at a time.**

Remember, your predicament does not predict your future. You always have the power of choice. Partnering with a Divorce Coach before, during, and after the dissolution of your marriage will enable you to navigate the process in a productive and empowered manner as you transition to the next chapter of your life. You have the capacity to soar! Be gentle with your soul and aim to show up authentically as you are. **There is only one you.**

YOU ARE EXCEPTIONAL!

*How will you set the intention of **moving forward in this moment**?*

_____

_____

_____

_____

_____

_____

_____

_____

_____

_____

_____

_____

_____

_____

_____

_____

_____

Replace criticism and comparison with acceptance and appreciation. You deserve love and affection!

About Jennifer Warren Medwin, MS, CDC

Jennifer Warren Medwin, MS is a CDC Certified Divorce Coach®, Certified Marital Mediator, and Supreme Court of Florida Family Mediator. Her private practice in Pinecrest, Miami is called Seeking Empowerment: Clarity through Partnership. Jennifer specializes in working alongside individuals and couples who are fearful of high conflict when contemplating divorce as well as those who hope to save their marriages. She partners with clients to develop the clarity, confidence, courage, conflict management strategies, and communication skills they need in order to move through the process. Jennifer uses her knowledge of coaching and mediation to help her clients emotionally prepare for the dissolution of their marriages or the reconciliation of their relationships in the most organized, time-efficient, and productive manner. Additionally, Jennifer is a member of the National Association of Divorce Professionals (NADP). She is also a contributing writer for Your Tango, Thrive Global, and OurFamily-Wizard. Her approach to Divorce Coaching and mediation provides clients with guidance and compassion through a difficult time in their lives.

Jen Warren Medwin MS, CDC
Certified Divorce Coach, Certified Marital Mediator, & Supreme Court of Florida Family Mediator

Seeking Empowerment:
Clarity Through Partnership
Work: 305-302-9777
jen@seekingempowerment.com
www.seekingempowerment.com

https://www.facebook.com/jenseekingempowerment
https://www.linkedin.com/in/jenseekingempowerment
https://www.instagram.com/jenseekingempowerment

Embrace the new. Exciting times are ahead!

Are You Ready to Feel Empowered?

You have the chance to write a new chapter in your book of life. Change is an opportunity for self-exploration and new beginnings. It can give birth to many possibilities to grow emotionally, physically, and spiritually.

I believe that the mindset you choose in the present moment will determine the type of divorce you will have and the direction your life will take you. Those who partner with me will be guided on a **path** to find their own sense of purpose, passion, and resolution.

I offer a 30-minute free consultation. During this time, you have the opportunity to explain the state of your marriage and your greatest needs, concerns, and goals. I will help you gain clarity about your current situation and provide insight into how to move forward.

Private one-on-one coaching is extremely beneficial. **Divorce is like a snowflake; no two are the same.** The outcome depends on many variables. Having an experienced partner to guide you through the divorce process is invaluable. You can schedule your free private consultation with me by emailing jen@seekingempowerment.com.

If you found this book helpful, please take the time to share it with others and leave a review on Amazon. This act will assist me in reaching more people looking for guidance if they are contemplating or going through the divorce process.

I am sending you so much support!

Jennifer Warren Medwin, MS, CDC

Accept compliments as they provide nourishment for your soul. Energize yourself!

Client Testimonials

"Jennifer pulled me out of progress paralysis and guided me to let go of the victim mentality…"

"After 22 years of marriage, 20 of which I did not work to raise our children, I was faced with the most challenging divorce. If I did not find Jennifer, I would not have survived. From our first meeting, she provided coping skills and support to rebuild my lack of confidence, pulled me out of "progress paralysis," and guided me to let go of the victim mentality. Jennifer provided a safe and respectful place for me to vent and laid the foundation for me to identify effective goals, develop time management skills, reclaim my power, and make real progress. During what was an extremely stressful and frightening time of my life, Jennifer listened intently. She shared her expert organizational skills, helped manage my legal team, encouraged self-care, showed empathy when I needed it, and assisted me in making wise decisions based on my case. Jennifer's immense dedication that I felt as her client was invaluable. She is someone I trust implicitly and will be forever grateful for."

-T.C.

"Jennifer was an amazing gift that literally walked me back to normalcy…"

"Jennifer is one of the most sensitive and understanding women I have ever met in my life. When I worked with her, I was going through some serious, life-changing challenges after my husband who is 43 had a heart attack and a stroke. I was devastated, hurt, lost, afraid, and just totally out of balance. Jennifer was an amazing gift that literally walked me back to normalcy. She helped me shift my perspective, motivated me to pick myself up again, and inspired me to do good things with my life. Jennifer is a unique woman, and I feel blessed to have been coached by her. I hope we never lose touch."

- P.F.

"Jennifer guided me, inspired me, and motivated me…"

"In going through my divorce, I faced so many obstacles that I never thought would come my way. With Jennifer by my side as my Divorce Coach, I was able to get through the end of my marriage. Jennifer helped me break everything down, and she supported me through the entire process. I would not have been able to move through the organizational, emotional, legal, and financial parts of my divorce without her by my side. I couldn't imagine going through this process without her. She guided me, inspired me, and motivated me to be the best version of myself. Jennifer taught me so many helpful skills and reminded me continuously that I only had control over my reactions and the present moment."

-R.G.

"Having Jennifer in my corner could not have come at a better time…"

"I am not a mushy person, but as I am walking through the trail at the dog park, I keep thinking about how meeting

Jennifer and having her in my corner could not have come at a better time in my life. Her words repeat in my head and keep me calm and focused."

- S.K.

"So grateful to have had the opportunity to work with Jennifer..."

"Jennifer helped me navigate my divorce, which was the most difficult time of my adult life. She provided an informative, calm, wise, loving space that allowed me to move through the process and redefine what my life could be like. Jennifer empowered me to have "a seat at the table." She will always have a seat at my table, and I am so grateful to have had the opportunity to work with her."

-M.R.

"Jennifer acknowledged my strengths..."

"It was a pleasure and an honor to have Jennifer as a coach. Through our weekly sessions, she helped me identify who I am as my best self. She acknowledged my strengths and challenged me to step out of my comfort zone. Through her coaching, I was able to identify new options. I truly appreciated her patience and her guidance. Jennifer is a compassionate listener and a great Divorce Coach."

- C.W.

*Appreciate the good
that exists in your
life because it will
fuel productive and
continuous momentum.
Practice gratitude!*

Acknowledgments

My deepest gratitude goes to my children, Jessica and Scott. Thank you for the joy you bring to my life. You mean everything to me! The love I have for you is immeasurable!

A big thank you to my dad who supported me in so many different ways before, during, and after my divorce. Even since his passing, he is helping me pursue my dreams.

My sincere appreciation to my sister and soul sisters, you know who you are, who have participated in my triumphs and lifted me up in my darkest of days. My life's journey is enhanced tremendously having all of you by my side.

A heartfelt shout out to Grandma Judi for loving me unconditionally and believing in me. You are one of my life's greatest blessings! I love you so much!

Many thanks to Marsha Cohen, my therapist, for helping me thrive and not just survive. Your guidance allowed me to tap into the strength, conviction, self-love, and hope that was buried underneath years of discontent.

My respect and admiration to my teachers and mentors at the CDC College for Divorce Coaching, Pegotty Cooper and Merry Berger. You taught me valuable information and have continued to support me both professionally and personally.

If you believe, you can achieve. Celebrate your essence because you are important!

Notes

Encourage yourself to turn your dreams into plans. You can do it!

Index

Index

Confidence is enhanced through education. Invest in knowledge!

Bibliography

American Bar Association - Dispute Resolution Process. (2013, January 17). Retrieved from American Bar Association: https://www.americanbar.org/groups/dispute_resolution/resources/DisputeResolutionProcesses/divorce_coaching/

CDC Divorce Training Intensive. (2020, May). Retrieved from Certified Divorce Coach: https://live-timely-8c94704ebe.time.ly/wp-content/uploads/2020/04/CDC-Brochure-May-2020.pdf

Clear, J. (n.d.). *How to Build New Habits by Taking Advantage of Old Ones.* Retrieved from Habits Academy: https://jamesclear.com/habit-stacking

Eddy, B. (2018). *Calming Upset People Fast with with EAR™.* Retrieved from High Conflict Institute: https://www.highconflictinstitute.com/hci-articles/calming-upset-people-fast-with-ear

Emerald, David. *"The Power of TED: The Empowerment Dynamic."*. (n.d.). Retrieved from https://powerofted.com/tag/empowerment-dynamic/

Gisondo, G. (2020, April). *In What Order Does the Court Handle Issues?* Retrieved from Gisondo Law: https://gisondolaw.com/in-what-order-does-the-court-handle-issues

Guys, F. L. (n.d.). *Conflicting Out Potential Attorneys in a Divorce or Family Matter.* Retrieved from Family Law Guys: https://familylawguys.com/conflicting-out-potential-attorneys-in-a-divorce-or-family-matter/

IACP. (International Academy Collaborative of Professionals). *What is Collaborative practice?* Retrieved from Collaborative Practice: https://www.collaborativepractice.com/what-collaborative-practice

Marguerite Manteau-Rao, C. (n.d.). *STOP and De-Stress In 30 Seconds.* Retrieved from Part of Mindfulness-Based Stress Reduction (MBSR) and other mainstream Mindfulness-Based: https://www.huffpost.com/entry/stress-reduction-technique_b_2750736

Marks, Rebecca. The Wellness Society.https://www.thewellnesssociety.org

Mind, C. Y. (2020, August). *What Is Habit Stacking? Create New Habits Using Current Habits.* Retrieved from Contact Your Mind: https://www.contactyourmind.com/blog

The National Law Review Volume X, N. 3. (2020, December 12). *Revisiting PEACE.* Retrieved from National Law Review: https://www.natlawreview.com/article/revisiting-peace

Weber, J. (2013, May 31). *Authenticity: Becoming Your True Self.* Retrieved from Health & Fitness.

Your empowered path awaits. There is no better time than today!

Many blessings as you demystify the big "D" and move forward.
Your future is yours to create!

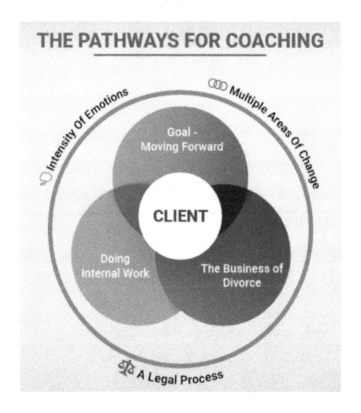

THE PATHWAYS FOR COACHING

Intensity Of Emotions

Multiple Areas Of Change

Goal - Moving Forward

CLIENT

Doing Internal Work

The Business of Divorce

A Legal Process

CPSIA information can be obtained
at www.ICGtesting.com
Printed in the USA
BVHW050058160323
660586BV00002B/4

9 781736 854402